So You Want to Be in

*A*DVERTISING

A GUIDE TO SUCCESS

WHAT TO STUDY, HOW TO PREPARE, WHAT TO DO ONCE YOU'RE THERE

ED CAFFREY

A FIRESIDE BOOK

PUBLISHED BY SIMON & SCHUSTER INC.

NEW YORK   LONDON   TORONTO   SYDNEY   TOKYO

A FIRESIDE BOOK
Published by Simon & Schuster Inc.
Simon & Schuster Building
Rockefeller Center
1230 Avenue of the Americas
New York, NY 10020
FIRESIDE and colophon are registered
trademarks of Simon & Schuster Inc.

Designed by Bonni Leon
Manufactured in the United States of America

1 2 3 4 5 6 7 8 9 10

Library of Congress Cataloging in Publication data

Caffrey, Ed.
So you want to be in advertising.
"A Fireside book."
1. Advertising—Vocational guidance.   I. Title.
HF5828.4.C34   1988   659.1'023'73   87-26497

ISBN 0-671-64590-0

*T*o my gentle lovely Markie

and to

David Bain

Brian Cauley

Mike Dabrowski

Ken Davis

Amanda Hahn

Jerry Harwood

Brian Hughes

Karen Kaczmar

Art Koch

Sallie Lee

Rosemary Love

Walter Lubars

Phil MacHale

Liz Reiss

Maria Romano

Al Silver

Sherry Valan

and especially

Joanne Casino

Thank you.

Contents

account people · studying for the business · the
variants of college instruction, some good, much
poor · how to steer your course to success and avoid
the wrong moves · making the rounds

gathering facts · research departments, large and
small · a big agency department, who does
what · research techniques · PROBE · testing
commercials · Burke Day-After · ARS · ASI Recall
Plus · focused groups · the computer people, fact
gatherers, vote counters · the changing industry · the
avalanche of new information · identifying prospects by
area, city and neighborhood · researching that critical
insight · what to study, how to prepare

how the media department came to be · media
planning · using the computer and using your
mind · what to study, how to prepare · media
buying · how TV time is purchased · the agency of
record · making it big or flopping · buying
services · breaking into buying

the least-defined position in the profession · several
sorts of creative people · conceiving a creative
idea · searching for a product advantage · determining
the brand's most persuasive aspect · ideating

· reasoning out from that persuasive aspect · getting the idea · working with a partner · presenting the work · writing a think piece · accuracy of layouts and storyboards · presenting print · presenting TV · the home-court advantage · presenting to creative director, account folks, client

9 PRODUCTION

from layout to photograph to magazine page · making magic · insisting on improvement every step of the way · selecting the photographer and the model · the preproduction meeting · making magic on the set · producing the ad · making commercials · film producers, agency and studio · getting a film together · production houses and directors · selecting talent · advertising music · the preproduction meeting · the role of creative supervisor · working with a director · editing the film · finishing and presenting

10 GETTING TO BE ONE

becoming a film producer · a haphazard route · college courses and training · looking for a job · becoming an art director or copywriter · a tale of two boroughs · employment agents · preparing your portfolio · choosing the right products · a diversion on legality

11 TEN CASES INSIDE ONE

selecting your portfolio · 10 product cases for you to

So You Want to Be in ADVERTISING

*F*IRST
*G*LANCE

*T*he 1986–87 Advertising Red Book records 3562 agencies in the United States. They come in all sizes and specialties from the big ten down to 2-person shops that may or may not be here for the 1987–88 edition. There are specialists in medical advertising, financial advertising, movie advertising, advertising in Arabic, Hebrew, Chinese, and three dialects of Spanish. Every single one of them, from J. Walter Thompson in Manhattan to Harold Flint in Fargo, is composed of the same three elements. There's someone to contact the client, someone to create the ads, someone to place the media. In tiny places, one of the first two doubles as the third. It's been that way since the beginning because that's the way it has to be. Advertising agents began as media middlemen, placing merchants' notices in newspapers and collecting a 15% fee. By the year of Lyman D. Morse's proud notice, 1898, the business had evolved to what it is today. He had clever writers to prepare copy and talented artists to illustrate it, he had experienced and competent account folks to contact his clients and knowledgeable media people to advise on the fitness of the media. Lyman D. Morse was a full-service agency.

The agency person who manages a client's business, day to day, is called the account person. An account person usually comes to the business from the study of marketing. It's a lengthy climb up the account stair of a large agency with steps called account coordinator, assistant account executive, account executive, account supervisor, management supervisor. At each step he or she will interface with someone on a corresponding step in the client organization.

The person who actually creates the ads is called the creative person and in fact is usually two persons, a copywriter and an art director. Writers and art directors partner up, sometimes for years, for good reason. They tend to see the sights of the world differently, and so bring two points of view to expression. An art director senses the colors and motion of the passing parade while a writer notes the order and progression. It's a partnership of mutual respect underlaid with a bit of mystique.

The art director is usually the product of an art school, usually having majored in advertising. You'll read a lot of usuallies in this text. That's because there are few forevers in this business, which is why we need so many experts.

The copywriter is almost always a liberal arts graduate, only sometimes an advertising major. He or she would probably have preferred writing books or movies and is almost certainly working on one.

The person who places the advertising in magazines and on television is called the media person. The media person has not gone to media school because there aren't any. He or she is usually a liberal arts

graduate who took a liking to the field of advertising but lacked marketing training or creative skills. Media is a training-on-the-job job that sorts out unfit folks fast. The surviving fittest go on to planning or buying, as we'll discuss.

Then there's research, an occupation that wasn't around in Lyman's day but is vital to any marketing operation today and growing more so. Research folks are born busybodies who enjoy learning why the rest of us do the things we do. Their degrees are as various as the media people's, with maybe a modicum more math.

There are other positions inside an agency—production and casting, for example. But they're not really attainable through college study.

Those 3562 agencies employ about 100,000 people. This book will talk about what those people do and how to go about getting to be one. Or how to improve your lot if you already are one. Ready? Here we go.

Starting Small

*L*et's start an advertising agency, you and I. You and I, Incorporated. You're the account person, I'm the creative person. That's just how many of the bigs of the business began. Take Young and Rubicam. Young was the account person, Rubicam was the creative person.

We have three little accounts and one big one. Friar's Department Store bills $400,000. That means Friar's will spend $400,000 on radio commercials, newspaper ads, and direct mail this year. And that means we'll make about $60,000 on the Friar's account this year. An agency is compensated either by fee or by commission, 15% on media and 17.65% on production expenditures. If it costs $1,000 to produce a Friar's radio spot, we earn $176.50. If the station charges $100 a minute to run it, we make $15 every time it runs. We'll charge Friar's a fee for the direct mail work, calculated on labor and overhead, marked up 25%. We'll charge our little clients a fee for all their work because their media spending is too small or too irregular.

All in all, we'll clear about $80,000 this year before taxes and expenses. That ranks us in the low minors of advertising (Young and Rubicam bills $3 billion), but it's not bad for an agency that's only 200 words old.

Friar's wants a new campaign. Lloyd, the marketing director, tells us that both he and Mr. Friar feel the need for something fresh and invigorating. It shouldn't have happened that way, of course. We should have been urging *them* into a new approach. A good agency anticipates client needs before they occur to the client. But we're still new and learning. It won't happen again.

Lloyd is an old-time retailer, 30 years in the department store business. It's a frequent condition, especially in smaller companies, that the marketing director knows very little about marketing or advertising. He came up through production or sales or finance and then one day was transferred over and given the title. The good marketing directors learn on the job. The other ones hire assistants. Lloyd has hired Diane, a young MBA from Northwestern University.

Today we meet in their conference room and talk about the new campaign. What is Friar's doing from their end? A new price policy, new designer lines, new décor? No, no, no. Nothing new. We press the point. It would help if the store could supply us with something unique to work with. Diane is sympathetic. Substance is a better marketing tool than slogans. But Lloyd shakes his head. Nothing new. The store is doing just fine just as it is.

Well, if the store won't give us anything new, we'll have to create the appearance of something new. That, by the way, is 90% of the job in the advertising business. Renew interest in an old unremarkable product by creating the appearance of something new and remarkable about it.

Let's start with the name. It's as good a place as any and it even works once in a while. Think of "All Tempa-Cheer" and "Gee—no, GTE." So, we start doodling:

> Friar's, make it a habit
> Brother, what a store
> Friar sale

At least there's something in the name to doodle about. Imagine if it were Kugel's. In our thinking we need to consider several applications for the new campaign. The idea should ideally be adept for radio and print advertising, point of purchase, direct mail, and employee relations. Point of purchase means the placards and posters you see in the store. Direct mail means those messages of urgency and excitement you find in your mailbox every day.

When you're hunting an idea like this, to fit several needs of a client's business, it's often productive to consider a personality. If it's serious business consider a real one, like Lee Iacocca or Cliff Robertson. If there's room for some fun consider a fanciful one, like Mr. Whipple or Ronald McDonald.

Friar's. Is there a real Mr. Friar? There is, but he's a bit of a stiff. Fanciful then . . . Friar Tuck? Friar Buck! A cute little cartoon Franciscan, chubby and cherubic. We'll make him gentle and innocent, naive to worldly ways. Not what you'd expect representing a mercenary retailer, but maybe we can use the anomaly to advantage. For our spring tool sale, we'll cartoon him building a birdhouse with his new Stanley hammer. For our summer lingerie sale, we'll show him averting his eyes from a lacy bra. On radio he can come in for a last-liner after we announce new money-saving values: "Heavens, that's good news!"

The campaign can be eye-catchingly effective, good fun, only slightly irreverent. Friar Buck emphasizes value and of course the store name. Does it meet the applicability criteria? Let's check. It works fine for newspaper and radio advertising, as we've seen. If we're clever at this, over the months folks will grow fond of our angelic cleric and they'll pay a bit more attention to mail with his image and likeness on the envelope. In-store? How about "Thou shalt not miss our shoe sale, second floor." The fun can extend to employee relations, with buttons or bulletin board posters. (Love thy customer?) Maybe even a Friar Buck balloon in the town parade.

Okay, we've got the idea. Now we execute. We hire a freelance artist to design the character for us, then draw up sample ads, store posters, employee materials, even the balloon. I write some sample radio spots and together we write a think piece. This is a vital element in the presentation of a new idea. Your most creative writing should lay out your thinking to the client. Ideally the client should be approving, even applauding, the idea before he sees the ads.

Diane does, Lloyd almost does. That is, he nods his head slightly. Tough sale, old Lloyd, and maybe a Methodist in the bargain. When he sees the advertising he nods twice. He has some reservations, but he'll show the work to Mr. Friar for his approval. Diane's ardent support will help. It is that way sometimes in a client relationship. In certain company systems the marketing manager, not the agency, presents to the corner office. That's a disadvantage since the marketing manager seldom has the presentation skills of the agency folk, nor the full conviction in the work. But Mr. Friar overlooks Lloyd's lacks and approves the advertising with compliments. He recognizes the effectiveness and the talk value of the campaign.

Now we go to work making and placing the material. We call back our freelance artist for tight comps of the newspaper and direct mail ads, as well as the point-of-purchase materials. A comp is an accurate pasted-up rendition of an ad, ready for the printer. We hold a casting session to discover the ideal innocent Franciscan voice and sign the bearer to a one-year contract with a one-year option. When you engage a personality, especially for television, you always seek to bind him or her with an exclusivity contract. The terms often extend beyond the airing of the campaign. After all, AT&T wouldn't want Cliff Robertson, after his contract ended, announcing that he'd switched to MCI.

We then produce the radio spots and buy the media time. There are several options for us in both areas. Radio spots are generally sold in 60- and 30-second lengths. In a medium-size city like ours there might be a half-dozen radio stations, AM and FM. Each station will have a unique constituency, consequent to its format. There may be a country-western station, an easy-listening station, a hard rock station, a light rock station, an over-fifties music-of-your-life station, a talk station, and a Mutual or CBS network station, for example. Each of these will glorify its statistics in offering its time to advertisers. The over-fifties station will cite the income of its listeners, call them decision makers. The talk station will insist its listeners are more "involved" than other audiences. One of the rock stations will probably have the highest rating, so it will stress numbers.

For Friar's we'll want a steady presence on two or three stations and occasional messages on most of them. It will depend on what we're selling. If it's appliances, we'll want the fifties and the talk, maybe the country, but not the rock. If it's bikinis, we'll choose both rocks but not the fifties. We draw up a media plan for print and broadcast, and present it to Lloyd and Diane. We've applied Friar's funds as cleverly as possible, we think, proposing a six-station buy of mostly 60-second spots and a scattering of 30s. Stations generally peg their prices on their listenership. One with a 10% share of audience will charge twice as much as one with a 5% share, broadly speaking. The time of day also influences the price of a spot. A minute in drive time, 7 to 9 A.M. or 4 to 6 P.M., will naturally cost more than a minute just before the prayer. We consider several cabalistic-sounding terms in selecting our purchases—reach, frequency, GRPs, CPM.

Reach = the number of individuals who hear your message. Frequency = the number of times they hear it. Reach × frequency = GRPs, gross rating points. Some advertisers consider *only* GRPs, and that's a mistake. The quality of the audience is equally important. Who's listening? Do the listeners match up with the product?

CPM means cost per thousand. How much does it cost to play your message to one thousand certified viewers or listeners? Four dollars? Eight dollars? Twelve dollars? Very generally speaking, for prime time television, between seven and eight dollars is considered good. Less is better, more needs a justification. Let's say that *Dynasty*, for instance, in 1986 drew a 22 rating. That's 22% of 19 million. Thirty seconds of advertising time retailed for $150,000. That's a CPM of $8.00. Good.

A show's rating refers to the percent of all TV homes, whether the sets are on or off. How many of those "on" sets are showing the show? The show's share refers to the percent of TV sets actually on that are tuned to the program. In a hamlet of a hundred homes, let's say 80 of the sets are lit, the other folks are bowling. Twenty-two of those sets are showing *Dynasty*. In that town, as nationally, *Dynasty* has achieved a 22 rating and a 28 share.

But. Though the sets are showing *Dynasty*, who knows how many eyes are watching *Dynasty?* More importantly for advertisers, who knows how many eyes continue watching the set when Krystle dissolves in tears and the picture dissolves to Cool Whip? Do you sit attentively through the commercial break? I'll bet you don't, and neither do the folks next door. Americans are developing uncanny timing skills, zapping out on the fade and back in on the super of the closing commercial, and what does that do to CPM? Assuming only half of those watchers have zapped or gone tinkling, the true CPM is more like $16. It's worse with sports, monumentally worse with the Super Bowl. Football watchers know exactly when the breaks of the game are coming and how long they'll last. One Super Bowl 30-second spot retails at $550,000 for an advertised CPM of $13.68. Heaven only knows the real cost, and that's about how high it is. The true facts of how many viewers are *really* watching the middle messages in a break cluster are still to be determined. For a long time it didn't seem that anybody was trying hard to find out.

• It's less drastic with radio, since fewer people physically tune out the commercials, but we Americans are equally gifted at tuning out mentally.

Inexact as it is, CPM is one measurement agencies use to suggest media to their clients. Others are reach and frequency. How many folks will one spot reach how often? Ideally you want to reach your people the right number of times. If you're announcing a clothing sale, how many times do you want your customer to hear your announcement? Twice? Three times? Five times? Probably no more than three—after that your clothing news wears out. So you calculate your media purchase accordingly.

There are some options in producing the radio as well. We'll want mostly sixties with some thirties to fulfill our media buy. But should they be live announcements or prerecorded? Or both? We can record Friar Buck opening and closing a spot with what's called a donut in the middle—silence to be filled by a live station announcer. For a client like Friar's the donut is a good approach, since no one knows exactly what the store will be featuring from month to month.

All right! Campaign conceived, executed, sold, and produced, media bought, we open a bottle of Mumm's. We're a success, you and I, and we're on the chase for additional accounts.

3

NEW
BUSINESS

*A*t an established agency, new business develops from two sources. Current clients account for half of it, assigning the agency new products. The other half is wooed and won in the open market. (It does happen that a new client walks in the door and says, "I like your work, please take my business," but that's as rare as Crystal Gayle's haircuts.)

› Here's how the wooing and winning works. The trade press announces that the A&B Corporation is severing its relationship with C&D

Advertising after 12 years and seeking a new agency. As coldly stated as a divorce notice and understating almost as much grief. Be sure that the last months of those 12 years were colored with anguish. Consider that partnership, over time. Company and agency together had seen the product through high times and low. Enduring friendships had developed at all levels on both sides, through countless lunches, filmings, outings, and conventions attended and enjoyed together. Then, like a marriage, the partnership began to fail. Why? Maybe it was:

1   A moribund product. To every brand there is a season. Short like the Edsel's or long like the Packard's, but one day gone with the rumble seat. It wasn't so long ago that folks rose to the music of their Philco radios, showered with Lifebuoy soap, donned their Oneita undies washed in Super Suds, had some Silvercup toast with a cup of Chase and Sanborn coffee while they read *Collier's* magazine. Then they brushed with Ipana, wound their Benrus watches, started up their Studebakers, and drove to work at W. T. Grant's. All of those companies had advertising agencies. As sales started to sour, company pressured agency to try a new approach. Failing that, a new one and a new one, on the notion that there must be some way to sell this stuff. Oh, the weekend presentations, the frenzied meetings, the fears. Finally, in desperation, the agency change was made.

2   Sinking stats. Think of Chrysler, think of Miller Beer. Both were headed for the museum unless a change was made. In Chrysler's case, a far more profound change than advertising alone could cause. In 1978, new chief exec Lee Iacocca presided over a woefully inefficient organization running out of cash, deteriorating factories producing boring out-of-date cars whose back doors popped open when they hit a pothole. Unit sales and share of market eroded by the month. The agencies felt the shudder of the quarterly reports. The same frenzied meetings, weekend presentations (make the word SALE bigger!), the same fears. Will we lose the account? Will I lose my job? Believe me, when stats are sinking, going to work becomes a sickening prospect. In the end Iacocca did remove

the business from Chrysler's two agencies, not for their failings but because he felt a new agency could work better with him in rebuilding the corporation.

Miller. Not so many years ago, when you could still buy a Benrus watch at Grant's, Miller was known as the champagne of bottled beer. The boys in the bar called it country club beer, lady beer. This was the era of national expansion for beers. Big names such as Budweiser and Schlitz were moving into everybody's local store at cut-rate prices and undercutting the local brands. Miller had the distribution to do it, but not the image. The boys didn't want lady beer at any price. If Miller failed to expand it was likely it would be swallowed whole by a growing giant as were Trommer's, Ruppert, and a hundred others, alas, no longer hiccuping with us. Fear, frenzy, pressure. Lights burned late at night as the agency–company relationship strained. Finally, in September of 1971, the trade press printed the notice. A month later the new agency announced the new campaign: "It's Miller Time." Miller Beer came out of the ladies' club into the steel mill. Sometimes there is some way to sell the stuff.

3 Complacency. Over the years the faces change in the company–agency picnic photo. Folks move up, move on, intentionally or not. It's said that, on the creative side, about three moves is right for a career. More about that further along. On the account side, a large agency will rotate assistants after a year, executives after two years, and supervisors after about three. Management supervisors book for the duration, barring conflict. It's similar on the client side, if the organization is big enough. Still, with all that movement, it's sometimes all too easy for the folks on both sides of the business to slip-slide into casual habitude. The weeks go by, sales are holding fine, the relationship is genial, management drowses at the wheel and never sees the danger signs. Suddenly one day, crash! The bimonthly sales report shows the business sagging badly. All indicators are down. How can it be? The last report showed that business was up! No, it showed that *dollar* volume was up slightly, behind a price increase, but *unit* volume was slightly down and

even that was disguised by a lag in factory shipment reports. Now the company will be forced to announce a third-quarter loss at least, and what's going to reverse the tide? The directors are furious, the agency's in trouble. As well it should be.

A good agency provides more than advertising. It must labor hard with a skeptical vigilance that anticipates sags and heads them off before they happen. Yes, the campaign seems to be working now, but when is it going to sputter? What do we have ready when it does? New executions, even a new strategy, tested and set to go?

But that is hard labor. It's so very much easier to loll along, present some more-of-the-same ads, then go for an early lunch, talk family and football, maybe a little business, the product's moving fine, maybe a little off due to weather or whatever, why fix something that isn't broken. . . .

4 Not invented here. Then there are instances when a perfectly healthy advertising campaign is trashed in favor of something not as good. When that happens look for a new arrival. Usually on the client side, usually a marketing director. The advertising on the air is selling, it's popular with the public, the sales force, the trade. There's only one trouble with it: It isn't his. (Sometimes hers, usually his.) Worse yet, it's credited to the last guy. What did management hire him for, to air the other guy's reruns? No way. He informs management that if they expect him to achieve his goals they'll support him in his demand for new and better advertising. And the agency better not drag its feet coming up with it or he'll damn well find another agency and maybe that's what he ought to do anyway.

So there. An agency that's done everything right is in serious peril of losing the business. It has happened, just that way. How to react? Bite your tongue and put an entire new group on the product, people untainted with the previous success. It hurts, but it sometimes saves the account.

5 The toiler who makes it to the top. When that occurs, beware, all you agency bigs who ignored him, even scorned him, all those years in his lonely cubicle. Jack, why don't you check this out with the lawyers? Jack, we need that report by 9 tomorrow. Jack, take care of this while we go to lunch. Then there comes a company picnic when those friendly senior client faces don't make it to the photo. There's Jack, all alone. Toiler Jack, newly resident in the corner office. Marketing Director Jack. How long will it be before Marketing Director Jack exacts his vengeance for all those years of slights? Bet on about six months.

Back in the rapid-pulse atmosphere of You and I, Inc., we've paused briefly for much-needed coffee and sweet rolls. But—prospects take note—even in these moments of repose, our minds are active. So it is that you, in midsip, notice a notice in the trade press: Rowan Office Furniture is splitting with Punim and Pupick Advertising after five years and seeking a new shop. Billings are estimated at $3 million.

Three million! That's a little beyond our current league, but what a jolt for our economy if we got it. Could we possibly get it? It's worth a try. We call Rowan's ad director and ask to join in the aspirants, citing our exemplary work for Friar's. "Why not?" he replies. "Make your presentation in two weeks."

The process goes someting like this. The director of marketing and his staff of two, let's say an assistant DM and a director of advertising, will hold court over a host of presenting agencies, known as the long list. Having heard a condensed proposal from each (qualifications, experience, staffing), the committee then pares the long list to a select few and asks those agencies for a more elaborate presentation, including strategic thinking and sometimes actual advertising. In our case, our qualifications, experience, and staffing are all too obvious, so we'll need to make the elaborate presentation on the first round.

What do we know about Rowan Office Furniture? Not much. What we do know is the guiding principle in winning a new account: Tell the management of the company something they didn't know or realize about their own business. It's not as impossible as it sounds, as we'll see. If you can achieve it, you stand clear of the other agencies who open with "Of course we'll have to learn the furniture business, but here's our latest work on orange juice." The prospect will realize he's dealing with aggressive minds bringing new thinking to his old problems, which is probably just what his other agency wasn't doing. It's also successful in new love affairs, by the way.

So we plunge into the subject of office furniture, learning the terms, the history, the trends, following leads, studying surveys and articles, analyzing the company's products and the competition's products. Over the years in this advertising business, you become expert in the damnedest things, one or two even useful in life.

We two aren't sufficient to the task, so we hire a professional researcher. There are such people and they're a big help in cases like this because they know just where to look and they're usually resourceful in following leads.

After four days of intense effort, we know the office furniture business better than anybody else who's not in it, and we even have a notion for that indispensable factor. It emerged somewhat from Rowan's own literature but more from several significant articles appearing not in the trade press but in women's magazines. The term is ergonomics. It refers to the interaction of people and utility objects, in this case office work stations. Office workers live large portions of their lives in the company of chairs, lamps, desks, and files. How those objects are designed to interact with legs, backs, eyes, and fannies is vital not only to the body owners but to the company owners. After all, a file clerk who hates her chair is going to be located in it far less than one who likes her chair.

And now a happy discovery. Reading through the articles we stop upon an organization called People Working. It's a league of office workers committed to ameliorating conditions in the workplace. They've run surveys, held seminars, and appeared on talk shows, urging on employers the plus and minus consequences of worker comfort. In red ink are sore eyes, aching backs, varicose veins, headaches, slowdowns, complaints, even lawsuits. But tranquillity, production, and profit reward the business manager who values people comfort over style and price.

We peruse the competitors' catalogues. Style and price. Comfort is mentioned down further, along with washability. The Rowan book and the Rowan ads mention comfort but never affiliate it with increased productivity.

There it is. The something the client didn't know or didn't realize about his own business. It never fails to impress the marketing committee. I've seen it happen. They look up, look at each other, then look at you and smile. Astoundingly, this new agency has produced thinking in two weeks that the former agency couldn't produce in 12 years. By the way, that invaluable element is even more valuable if it leads to increased profit, because that is the bottom-most line in business, and ours will.

Several questions remain:

Will the furniture support the campaign?

Will People Working endorse it?

What will the ads look like?

Are there any additional ideas that could cherry the icing on the cake?

We can answer the first two at the same time. The chapter president of the New York People Working agrees to meet us at the Rowan showroom in New York. Travel and expenses will nick us $300 but that's what we'll spend on cocktail napkins if we get the account.

"Excellent" is what she pronounces Rowan furniture, and she points out why. The chairs support the body through several posture changes, which is the way people sit through several hours. The color elements of the work station are more than harmonious, they are easy on the eyes and soothing on the mind. The location of drawers and files minimizes both walking and bending.

Will People Working endorse Rowan? She can't comment for the organization but the chapter will. After all, they can use the publicity too.

We lay out three ads, each emphasizing one advantage of a Rowan work station. They're titled Back Happy, Eye Happy, and Foot Happy, and each features a prominent plug from People Working. We now think out our think piece, and as we do a new thought surfaces. Home offices. Millions of American homes now have private work stations. Computer, word processor, some sort of filing system. Chances are, folks simply pull up a kitchen chair and go to work. Why not a Rowan chair? Why not a Rowan home work station? Expansion of attention to the home means consumer ads as well as trade ads, maybe even television. And that means expansion of ad budget to $5 or even $6 million. Seems we now have cake, icing, and cherry too. We're ready to present.

There are times, in new business go-rounds, when the fix is in. One agency, possibly even the incumbent, is preferred by the DM, and only scandal or miracle will alter the outcome. This is not one such time. Monday's advertising columns read: "Tiny agency selected for Rowan Furniture."

We open a bottle of Dom Perignon.

4

*F*ULL *S*ERVICE

*T*his first celebration is for us alone. You and I together in our small but homey office, with sketches of a portly friar and ergonomic chairs overhanging the dartboard. We reflect on how far we've come how fast, farther than some come in a lifetime. In the glow of our private exultation, we plan our public party. An extended family wingding it will be, part ardent felicitation and part cold publicity. Diane will be there, chatting with the Rowan ad manager. Relatives, friends, the man from the newsstand, anyone who's wished us well along the way, they'll all be there. We'll introduce Lloyd to your mother and to Franco of Franco's Verona Garden, our first client. Lloyd has met the Rowan DM at regional marketing seminars. Business writers from the local papers will sup on egg rolls and white wine and tomorrow print portions of our press release. A roving photographer will snap us with the Rowan team and we'll forward that photo to *Ad Age, Adweek,* and the furniture trade publications. A hot shop is only hot when the industry feels the heat.

Soon afterward Rowan will hold a plant tour and reception for us. We'll be escorted through the factory wearing hard hats, meeting section managers, taking notes and names. The designers and engineers we want to speak to won't be at the plant but they will be at the meet-the-new-agency reception that evening. In fact, nearly everybody on the payroll will be there, finance and production people, salesmen and secretaries. It's a free party and they'll be mildly curious about us.

A pause about all these parties. There do be a lot of them in this business and I guess that sounds enticing until you stop to reason why. Advertising is an exceedingly unpermanent profession. Almost all accounts change agencies sooner or later. An agency with fifteen accounts can count on losing at least one during the year, winning one or three or none. People move in and out of jobs, in and out of agencies, even in and out of the business. The same agency's phone directories from 1980 and 1986 would read like two different companies'. There is no job security, no certain pension, contracts only at the highest level. The only insurance policy is talent, and even that has clauses. Maybe that's why advertising people are always taking pictures. In every issue of *Ad Age* there are scores of photos of adlanders partying together, golfing, dancing, sipping chardonnay together. Nearly every office has mounted glossies of its occupant together with colleagues and clients at an outing or filming, preferably embracing a celebrity. It's all so transient they need to memorize the moments.

There'll be those at the Rowan reception who'll size us against their previous agency buddies and quietly conclude that a gross mistake has been made. Most will realize that a change was needed and give us the benefit of a fresh start. One of their first questions will concern agency staffing. Our answer will be we're looking. In fact we are. You and I now need to become what we've always hoped we would be—a full-service agency. We're looking for:

1 A media person. Friar's needs newspaper space and radio time. Rowan's needs trade magazine and newspaper space, and if we're successful, consumer magazine space and maybe even television.
2 A research person. We'll be proposing consumer surveys as well as ad testing for both clients.
3 An art director. There's plenty to do on both accounts and even Franco wants a new ad for the Verona Garden's new Terrace Bar.
4 A mailroom and copier person. Probably a retired city fireman.
5 A secretary–receptionist–mother hen.

How do we find 1, 2, and 3? We advertise in the advertising press. Here's a selection of ad ads from *Ad Age* (see next page).

Notice one common factor about all eight agencies. They're all out of town. In advertising, out of town means not in New York. Chicago and Los Angeles folks will jeer that, but it is the solemn truth. Just about everybody wants to work in New York. With reason. Almost all the main offices of almost all the main agencies are located in Manhattan, though no longer on Madison Avenue. Almost all the big campaigns of almost all the big clients are done out of those New York offices. Big campaigns mean big awards, big money. Almost all but not all. Chicago agencies do Allstate, McDonald's, even Charlie the Tuna. Bartles and Jaymes is done out of Hal Riney's splendid shop in San Francisco. Those big-budget Bud spots are done in St. Louis. Every year, dazzling commercials and ads from Tucson and Minneapolis agencies are entered in the big festivals and many win awards.

And yet, show those want ads to an out-of-work Manhattan art director, even one who's been hunting for six months. Watch his head shake as he reads them. Atlanta maybe, maybe even Milwaukee, but Omaha? Secaucus?

Let's check it from your point of view. Assuming a career of three different agencies, why not make the first or second an out of towner? Consider the relative advantages, both as first and second agency.

WE'RE ASKING FOR THE MOON BUT WE'LL SETTLE FOR TWO STARS.

We're a 4A Milwaukee agency looking for an art director with 5 years agency experience (including financials, please) and a copywriter with 3 years agency experience. All we request is unflagging dedication, speed and brilliance. And six non-returnable samples of your niftiest work—along with your price tag—sent to Ernie Monroe.

KLOPPENBURG SWITZER & TEICH INC. ADVERTISING
1749 North Prospect Avenue,
Milwaukee WI 53202

"Who me? Move to Omaha?? Nebraska???"

Yes, you! Sit back for a moment and imagine that you live in Omaha, Nebraska.

Your money goes a whole lot further. You can afford to live in a better house. Your children go to better schools. Taxes are lower. You don't commute. The air is clean. The crime rate is low.

Culture? The Community Theatre is nationally recognized. Broadway Roadshows play the Orpheum. The Joslyn Museum gets the major travelling art exhibits. The Omaha Symphony can hold a candle to its counterparts in Minneapolis and St. Louis. Stars from Bruce Spring-

All-expense paid week-end for two in beautiful Omaha.

We'd like to give you a trial-size package of the good life in Omaha. We want you to see for yourself, experience for yourself what it would be like to live and work here. So, if your samples and resume interest us, we'll pay all expenses to bring you and your wife, husband, boyfriend, girlfriend, mother or whatever to Omaha to check it out. We need you if you are one of the following, with five years agency experience —

Art Director – strong in print and T.V.
Copywriter – strong in broadcast, eat in print.
roadcast producer – good chnical knowledge plus ability to ntribute creatively.
nd resume and six samples of ur best to Bev Miller, Personnel rector, Bozell & Jacobs, 10250 gency Circle, Omaha, NE 68114. o phone calls, please!

CREATIVE COPY CHIE[F]

New Jersey's fastest growing and most creative shop needs a Copywriter who can conceive and execute innovative, eff... campaigns. Our ideal chief is also strong on administration and contact and has consumer/package goods experience. Beer and experience helpful. Broadcast experience a definite plus.

We are a division of Glover Advertising, Inc., one of the cou... most respected point of sale/sales promotion companies. We o... salary commensurate with experience and a comprehensive b... package. Contact **David Morgasen** at (201) 867-5800.

500 County Ave., Secaucus, NJ 07094

RESEARCH DIRECTOR

San Antonio advertising agency seeking candidates for newly established position of research director.

Advanced degree in business or social sciences with at least 2-3 years experience in market research in an advertising agency or the marketing department of consumer products company.

Should have experience in collecting and analyzing secondary research.

Should have primary research experience including questionnaire design, survey methods, statistical analysis and report writing.

Should have strong, analytical skills, statistical competence, and excellent written and verbal communication skills.

Send resume to: Stephen Plum, Senior Vice President, The Pitluk Group, 45 N.E. Loop 410, San Antonio, Texas 78216.

GROUP CREATIVE DIRECTOR

Growing Southeastern agency has an excellent opportunity for an experienced art director to function as group creative director and lead two bright young writers and fine designer/art director. Must have a good advertising reel and book. Our creative product has won major national as well as international recognition. Good client list to work with. Let us see a few pieces of your more recent work.
.O. Box 5806, Columbia, SC 9250

Atlanta Agency Seek[s] Experienced Media Dir[ector]

We are a strong, aggressive, $20 million agency on ... move, with an excellent opportunity for an experienced media director who would like to contribute to and participate in our exciting forward progress.

Our agency needs a vibrant professional with in-depth and varied planning and buying background in all media, from network TV to trade print.

We are seeking an exceptional individual, combining ambition and maturity, to assume the leadership and responsibility for a well respected, widely experienced department. Our media director will be expected to work closely with our account service and creative leadership, as well as with an outstanding group of clients and prospects.

An innovative strategic planner with the ability to make knowledgeable, "on-target" recommendations in writing and in presentations, is essential.

We are an agency in a hurry. So if this sounds like the opportunity you want, send us your resume soon. Because when we find the person we want to be our media director, we are going to move in a hurry.

Send resume and salary range to Merrill Williams, Executive Vice-President/Administration.

LILLER NEAL, INC.
Advertising, Public Relations and Direct Marketing
2700 Cumberland Parkway, Suite 200
Atlanta, Georgia 30339
Member American Association of Advertising Agencies

TRAFFIC MANAGER/RICHMOND

An opportunity to join a group of advertising professionals, and to manage the workflow of an exciting, growing agency.

Good starting salary, benefits and a liveable city that's close to the beaches and Blue Ridge Mountains.

Necessary to have solid experience in traffic management.

Please send a summary of your background to:
Brad Armstrong, President
Stuart Ford Incorporated, 1108 E. Main Street, Richmond, VA 23219.

SFI
STUART FORD INC[ORPORATED]

Write Now.

We need a hot, seasoned writer who writes well, writes fast, right away.

Send us a letter, your resume, and some samples you may never see again. A variety of consumer and business-to-business ads and collateral is preferred. Photocopies acceptable.

GwynnAdvertising Inc
329 Two Gateway Center, Pittsburgh, Pennsylvania 15222

''OUT OF TOWN'' AGENCIES, MEANING NOT IN NEW YORK.

First agency. Where do you live? Central Missouri? There are 83 agencies within 150 miles of you, principally in St. Louis and Kansas City. You send every one of them a letter and a résumé. Twelve of them respond, they'd like to meet you. Over the next two weeks you interview with all 12, improving your technique as you go. Promises to keep you in mind but after two more weeks, still no sale. You widen your circumference to 300 miles, netting 56 more agencies in Memphis, Des Moines, Little Rock, Topeka, and—Omaha! Letters again (better this time) and résumés get you ten responses. Back behind the wheel for round two of interviews, but on this round you score. An Omaha agency hires you, starting next week. It's taken you about six weeks and cost you a few hundred dollars. Compare that process to the New York experience.

If you don't live within a few hours of midtown, you'll either have to make several overnight voyages here or move in. I know what you've heard about New York, about the rents, the traffic, the parking, the grime and graffiti, and I guarantee it's not true. It's considerably worse. So you sublet one room at $900 a month and send off letters to the bigs. You get maybe four replies. It's a tough town. Smiles but no sale on the interviews, 20 more letters to the nearly bigs. Five replies, again no sale and the rent's due. Six months later and $6000 poorer you finally hit. Hit me if you want for exaggerating but the point is valid. The competition is ferocious. It reminds me of a Casey Stengel story. Scene, spring training. A big bonus pitcher just out of high school is starting his first game in the pros. Single, double, walk, single, home run. Casey calls time, ambles out to find a very dazed young man. "I can't understand it," the kid says. "In high school every game I pitched was a one-hitter, a two-hitter. . . . " Casey nods, says, "Remember the guys who got the one hit, the two hits? They're all here."

Same thing in New York advertising. They're all here.

There's no disputing Omaha's advantages in parking, pricing, or paucity of perpetrators, nor New York's in ballet, Broadway, and big-league baseball. The only question is, how will this first job set you up for your second?

The Omaha agency will almost certainly have fewer people and smaller clients. That will probably mean greater lateral movement for you, sooner. You'll become more deeply involved on several businesses, fattening your chances for success stories. Success stories at agency one are the credentials you need for a lucrative leap to agency two, with a bold-type footnote, as we'll see.

The same thing might happen in New York (we have hundreds of small agencies here, too), but more likely not. As a rookie you might spend two years on one or two large accounts. They may or may not be success stories, and even if they are you'll have difficulty claiming credit. Mediocre credentials for a lucrative leap. However, you are a part of it, New York New York, so you take advantage. You wake up in this city that never sleeps (who could, with the truck horns and police sirens?), and you concentrate on getting out of dead-end agency one and starting over in promising agency two.

One other advantage. If your advertising is good and it runs in New York, you're a half stride ahead of somebody whose good advertising runs in Nebraska—just because the agency-two hirer will have seen and admired yours.

Unless agency two is in Omaha, and that may not be a bad idea. Consider.

You started in New York. It's now time for that lucrative leap and your résumé is only okay. (We'll delineate proper preparation for creative and marketing job-hunting further on.) The big-city positions open to you are therefore only okay. Not what you want for a long career or as a setup for agency three. Look over those out-of-town ads again. They're sometimes willing to overlook an imperfection. And there is that wider range of smaller clients, the opportunity to swing a little freer and be directly responsible for success. Then again, you might just love it and stay for a lifetime.

Now it's time for that bold-type footnote. Is an out-of-town success story the credit you need for a New York job? It depends on what your job is and what the account is. If you're a writer or art director, it almost doesn't matter what products are the subjects of your ads. The quality of the work greatly outweighs the class of client. Any big-agency creative director will understand, looking over an array of dazzling ads, that these are the subjects you had to work with and you worked wonders with them.

Untrue in marketing. As an account exec or brand manager you'll probably have served on only one product. You may have single-handedly doubled the business, but what sort of business was it? If BBDO has a similar client, you have a chance for a job. Especially if New York candidates are scarce. Fast food is a category in point. If you are a hot property with McDonald's and a New York agency has just won a fast-food account, they'll pay your ticket. On the other end are agricultural accounts and stores. Airlines are high, along with cars and beers, and banks if they're big. But you will have to stay in your category and maybe drop a grade for starters.

You and I place our ads and wait for our answers. We're impressed with three or four aspirants, so we invite each of them for a mutual look-see. Some we turn down and some turn us down, but we're quite pleased with the three we hire.

You and I are/is a full-service agency.

5

ACCOUNT WORK

*N*ow let's talk about you. The real you this time. You like the sound of those account titles: account executive, account supervisor, account management. They announce that the agency marketing department is the primary line of agency activity. Indeed it is. We on our creative track run parallel to the mainliners in spurts, often exceeding their speed, but in the long run it's the account folks who run the account. That is the way it must be, structurally. A manufacturer may produce a fine product, but as fine as it is, a product rarely sells itself these days. Only fine marketing sells products, fine or otherwise. So the manufacturer forms a marketing department, which in turn engages the services of an advertising agency. The agency marketing department becomes, in effect, the longer marketing arm of the manufacturer. Of course then, account management is the agency's main line.

Which is not to say that account folks are the best paid or the best known or lead the best lives. On a year-for-year basis copywriters often earn more money, and crack media buyers earn a lot more. Account work is largely an anonymous and stressful profession, but such is the executive life in any line.

A day in the life? It might begin with a call to your cocaptain, the brand supervisor. Titles and duties will vary a degree or two, depending on the size of the client and the size of the agency, but for an average big client at an average big agency, the cocaptains of the entire procedure are the client brand supervisor and you, the agency account supervisor. All the component parts function through you two. She at her end, let's say she's a she, confers regularly with her company's marketing management, sales people, research and development people, and with you. You confer regularly with the agency media people, research people, creative people, and with her. She sometimes meets with your people, you sometimes meet with hers. You two, in tandem, captain the product through the year. (Eventually you'll move off onto another product in the agency and she'll move off onto another product at the company.) Through the year there'll be sales meetings to receive input from the field; there'll be meetings with a market research firm like Nielsen where you'll learn how the product is faring on the shelf; and there'll be budget meetings to determine how much the company will spend to advertise the brand this year.

Have you paused to wonder how a company decides how much money to spend to advertise its product? Well then, let's pause to explain. There are two accepted formulas, both inexact and, like everything else in advertising, rife with usuallies.

The first is called A to S, advertising to sales. How much of a product's sales revenue does the manufacturer invest in advertising? The range is wide, from less than 1% to more than 20%, and it varies by category. A product's A to S ratio is usually pegged on the degree to which advertising is responsible for its sale. Retail stores are down around 3%, toys about 12%, detergents up to 15%, and cosmetics over 20%. It does, in fact, make a general sort of sense. Take two examples. How much does advertising influence your choice of a retail store? Not as much as location, I'd wager. If there's a Penney's in your nearby mall, you're a Penney's shopper. If the Penney's were a Sears, you'd be a Sears shopper. That's excluding specials, year-end clearances, and the like, when you might drive five miles more for a big item, and that's why such stores save their advertising dollars for such events.

Not so with detergents. Cheer, Tide, and Ajax are all located on the same shelf, they all cost about the same, excluding promotions, and they all wash out about the same amount of dirt. Why then do folks have favorites? Why do you favor one detergent? Because you have the impression that, somehow, it's better than the others. Most of that somehow is made of advertising. Same with floor cleaners, dishwashing liquids, shampoos, and toothpastes. As George Wallace said about his opponents, there ain't a dime's worth of difference among 'em; yet you have a favorite in every category. Advertising. Detergent makers feel they must spend 15% of their sales dollars to keep that somehow going.

The formula follows form in most categories, but far from all. You'd think that car makers, whose sales lean so heavily on image, would be up in the double digits. They're down around 2. And soft drinks? You'd think that Coke and Pepsi, the all-time competitive super bowlers, whose sales depend almost *entirely* on image, would have an A to S of 50. Nope, only around 8. But that 8 represents many many millions of dollars. About $900 million, all told, by both corporations.

Here you wonder, while we're on the subject of colas and dollars, about those multimillion-dollar contracts colas have given to rock stars and athletes. Can Michael Jackson really be worth $15 million of Pepsi Cola's ad budget? All right, that's worth a clause within our pause.

Both Coke and Pepsi have about an 18% share of the soft-drink market. Every share point is worth about $200 million, so everything and anything that either of them can do to shift a point its way is worth a try. Both realize keenly, through trying and erring, that their market, our youth, is constantly renewing itself and constantly responsive to what's new. Recall that when Michael Jackson was new he was an item of awe. This gorgeous androgynous biracial creature held an almost mystical sway over our youth, our black and white boys and girls. Was it worth rendering unto Michael $5 million, then $10 million of Pepsi's $150 million annual ad budget? Not a dime's worth of doubt about it. Or about Lionel Richie's $8 million or Doctor J's $2.5 million from Coke, or for that matter, Bruce Willis's who-knows-how-many millions from Seagram's.

Second clause within the pause. Wine coolers, one of the fastest-growing categories in the beverage business, were thriving in 1985. The list of entrants had swelled to about 120. Everyone in the industry realized that was far too many, that the attrition body count would be wicked. Only a dozen or so brands would survive, and the survival race was on. The front-runner was California Cooler, with about 30% of the market, but Bartles and Jaymes was making a hard run at them. Seagram's, a distant fourth, had just developed a genuinely superior-tasting cooler, but this far into the contest, how were they going to attract folks' attention to it? They bought something that folks' attention was already avidly attracted to, something called Bruce Willis. The immediate attention that Bruce Willis brought to Seagram's Golden Cooler was literally priceless, because it probably could not have happened any other way.

Postscript: At this writing, Hal Riney's grand old geezers, Bartles and Jaymes, have blown past California Cooler into first place (thank you for your support). Seagram's is now running third and looking healthy.

There are several advertising situations where you might consider looking into familiar faces. If your product is loping along back in the herd of faceless also-rans, for instance. Think of the attention John Houseman brought to the prestigious but pallid house of Smith, Barney. All he really says is that they *urrn* it, but over time you come to assume that Smith, Barney is like John Houseman—crusty but clever and exceedingly cautious with your money. Which is just what they want you to assume and which is why the right celebrity is often worth a lot of company money. The product benefits from personality transference.

Faceless, formless AT&T takes on the face and form of Cliff Robertson, handsome, sincere, upright Cliff Robertson. He's worth whatever they pay him, because his very person has given AT&T validity.

There are several noteworthy cases where successful symbol–spokesmen aren't actors or even humans, but a tiger, a lion, and a teddy bear. Inside your gas tank the Exxon tiger roars. In the chasms of the financial kingdom the Dreyfus lion stalks—powerful, intimidating, Lord of the Street. Both products benefit from the personality transference. But the envelope for Best Use of a Symbol–Spokesman, Fictional, has to go to the Snuggle teddy bear. Have you seen the commercials? A cuddly teddy explains the virtues of Snuggle fabric softener in a wittoo-bitty teddy voice. Every mother has had at least two teddy bears in her life—one when she was a baby and one for each of her own babies. Every baby knows what a teddy bear means. It means security, it means love, it means softness. What nice virtues to transfer to a fabric softener. That wittoo-bitty teddy has built Lever Bros. a $300 million business.

Where were we? Right, the second formula for fixing a budget. It's called share of voice. How much is your competitor spending to advertise his product? You home in on his spending rate and adjust yours accordingly. Let's say he has 20% of the market and you have 10%. He's spending $10 million to maintain his 20 share, you're spending $5 million to attain your 10. In this upcoming year, you judge that he'll raise his spending to $15 million, hoping to increase his share. That means he'll be outshouting you by 3 to 1 instead of just 2 to 1. That means you'll have to hike your budget to $7.5 million just to balance the comparative decibel level. Or are you prepared to attack *his* share points? You'll need to speak even louder then. Nine million? Ten? Twelve? That's share of voice. And now, back to you, account supervisor, and your client cocaptain.

There'll be copy presentations and media presentations where your copy or media supervisor will have done most of the work and will do most of the presenting, but you will ensure that the work is sold because you and only you see every piece of the picture. At our Friar's presentation, I presented the Friar Buck ads and radio spots, but you did the preview and the review and the overview. You were ready with answers because you knew what questions were coming. Has a friar ever been used in advertising? How does the public feel about clerics? How much time and money will it take to develop Friar Buck as the store's symbol? Will the church complain? You knew. You'd checked your sources, from *Ad Age* to the archdiocese, and you had the answers. Diane asked different questions than Lloyd asked, better ones, but you anticipated all of them.

It's always the way. If you know the players, you'll know their questions. Know the players. It's an important piece. Play to all of them, but primarily to the power player.

All in all you'll be spending a great deal of time dealing with your client cocaptain, on the same or opposite sides of the table. You'll be spending about an equal amount of time dealing with your colleagues.

Your media supervisor, for example. Working with a predetermined budget and market target, the media group prepares a multimedia plan for the year. Do you feel they've made the most of the money? Do their suggestions manifest genuine thought and daring or merely computer efficiencies? Do you anticipate any flak from your client, the brand supervisor? Or your agency creative supervisor? Should you propose a higher spending-level test for one market? You'll be dealing with media several times a month.

Which will be when you're not dealing with research. The Nielsen audits will tell you how many units are moving through the check-outs, but they can't tell you if consumers are changing their attitude about your product. They can't tell you how well viewers like your TV advertising. The agency research department can. Your account research director (ARD) will structure a survey to determine anything you need to know about the brand or the market. But research surveys cost money. Is this proposal too expensive? Will the client go that high? Are the questions phrased to elicit all you need to know? How will the creative and media supervisors feel about the proposal? Can the ARD fit this study in ahead of others he's working on if you get the okay right away? You'll be dealing with research on and off all year.

Unless you're dealing with creative, and that is the biggest deal of all. Account and creative. Or should I say account versus creative? It is, potentially and frequently, the most difficult relationship in the business. But not always, and certainly less frequently these days. Confused? Good. So are the rest of us. Imagine a jigsaw puzzle that the cat knocked off the table and you can't locate eight pieces. That's how hard it is to put together a coherent image of this rocky rapport, especially for someone like me who's been so personally involved with it all these years. Let's commence with the then of it and work our way forward to the now of it.

Years ago, 50, 40, 30, even 20 years ago, there bestrode the advertising world like colossi a species of giants called troglodytes. Troglodytes were account biggies who regarded their accounts as private fiefs. They were highly connected at the top of the client organization, with at least as much influence there as the client's own marketing people. The troglodyte dined, golfed, and vacationed with his giant client crony. Their families spent holidays together. At the agency he spoke for the client, infallibly. If J.T. didn't like a campaign, it didn't go to the client. Never mind how brilliant it was, how right it was, how hard everybody worked on it, if J.T. didn't like it, it didn't go to the client. And J.T. might not like it for a lot of reasons, some logical. Maybe it was funny and J.T. saw no place for humor in advertising. Maybe it involved a woman presenter and J.T. sneered that no woman ever sold him anything. These are, by the way, real examples.

As J.T. spoke for the client, his account staff spoke for J.T. Meaning that any rookie account assistant could turn down an ad. It was pointless for the creative supervisor to take issue with him because the account assistant would simply take the issue up his hierarchy and 10 minutes later the creative supervisor would receive a phone call from *his* boss urging him to do it their way and in the future to try to be more cooperative.

These troglodytes are gone from the landscape today, brought low by their own intractability. In the late 1960s, business schools began graduating a new breed of marketing major—smarter, less smug, more aware and open-minded, and to J.T.'s horror, often female.

When they arrived on the agency scene, they were appalled at the attitudes. How can reason prevail in this czarist autocracy? The brand clearly requires an overhaul—new ideas, a new strategy, a new look. But His Eminence in the corner office prefers things his way, as they are, and won't surrender one point of his prerogative. A similar attitude adjustment was taking place in the client organization. As the new marketers there moved ahead in power they took vociferous objection to the arrogance of their own corner giants. The people at the top of this company, they said at both companies, are crippling its abilities. So down came the trogs and oh, what a fall was that. J.T. got the axe! Followed by a chorus of whispered hallelujahs.

Today's account folks are by far the brightest, deftest, easiest to work with and like, ever to enter the business. A primary factor is that they enter from a diversity of backgrounds. There are as many liberal arts grads coming in now as business grads, as we'll discuss.

Caution: The troglodyte is not extinct. There is a new variety equally as arrogant and domineering as the old, but far abler, far more subtle about it. Handle with extreme care.

Okay, smart and likable account supervisor, you're dealing with the creative folks. If they're good ones, then they're always ahead on the work. If not, if they're inept, then you've got trouble in your business life. Nothing is more trying to agency–client harmony than creative work that's behind schedule and not worth waiting for when it gets there. But such is not your karma. You and your creative supervisor function well together. You two confer with your client cocaptain regularly to plan next moves. A new strategy? The use of new media? A new executional format? A new song? If you truly work well with each other then you'll think through the new work together and your thoughts will be impressed in his ideas.

Now wouldn't you suppose that's the way anyone would want to proceed? It's so practical, so productive. But it ain't necessarily so. Another hangover from the age of confrontation is the creative attitude of "Just give me the assignment, I'll get back to you in a week or so." There are still today, in the halls of creation, too many art directors and writers suffering from this delusion. As a copywriter I want to know all you know about the subject. I want to volley some facts and notions back and forth with you, and while we're volleying, some thoughts will occur, maybe the same thoughts to both of us. Then and only then will I walk the lonely corridor to my solitary cell, but chances are what I come out with will be on target, on strategy, and legal, and chances are you'll like it because you had a piece of what went into it. Meantime the deludeds could as easily emerge with something that misses not only the target but also the door the target is nailed to.

And how do you judge a creative idea after all? I hereby offer you a How To and a How Not To. The second first.

1 As the creative presentation is being made, try to spot the errors. Take notes.
2 Begin your response by enumerating the mistakes.
3 Check the work against the written strategy. Are all the points covered? Are they correctly weighted?
4 Suggest how missing points might be included. To assuage feelings, begin your comments with, "I'm no copywriter but . . . "

Please. I implore you. NEVER DO IT THAT WAY. Do it this way:

1 Listen attentively. Make sure you understand the work. If not, ask for clarification.
2 Imagine you're not seeing it here in the office but home in your chair. See it as an uninvolved viewer or reader. DO YOU LIKE IT? The rest is commentary.
3 If you like it or if you don't like it, say so. I love it. I hate it. Creative people would far rather hear that than "It's not bad, if we could only change four or five things."
4 If you love it but it's a little off strategy, can it be amended? If not, can the strategy be amended?
5 If you hate it, why? Way off strategy? Illegal? Boring?
6 If it's boring chances are you won't hate it, chances are you'll just remain unmoved by it. Please realize that boringness is a more grievous sin than off-strateginess. The off-strategy storyboards die

in conference. The boring boards often live on and become commercials nobody watches, costing uncountable time and money and maybe the account.

If you love the work, call your client cocaptain and arrange for a presentation. Do a little preselling.

If you don't love the work you'll need to call your cocaptain and explain the situation. Regardless of your explanatory abilities, the delay is going to cause consternation. It has to. The timetable of events, meetings, copy presentations, production, was established in consultation with all, and now all depends on it. There are no time-outs left. The copy needs to be right on schedule.

Well, here you ask, as I used to, loudly, how can that be practical? The creative process doesn't resemble an exact science. What if inspiration doesn't strike by Wednesday at four? True, but inspiration can be ushered along. Thorough discussion between creative and account people is not just a good idea, it is imperative. It maintains inspiration's sights on the center of the target. And you, account supervisor, need to gauge your creative group's time requirements. Are they brilliant but slow? Allow time. Not so brilliant but slow? Allow more time. Leave room for revision. There isn't much you can do beyond that, except, well, prayer is said to have its merits.

So as you see, account work wants a high degree of mastery of several skills—marketing, presenting, planning, writing, administration, diplomacy, and selling. The skill of skills? Selling. You're forever selling, to your clients and your colleagues. And forever thinking about that product, whatever it is: Chevrolet cars, Dial soap, Smucker's Jam. Smucker's Jam eats you for breakfast. It's on your mind on the plane, on the phone, over lunch, until your tour is ended and you move to another brand. The product is as consuming as you let it be, and you want to let it be, to a defined extent. Some account folks let it extend deeply into their lives, taking the office home every night in a bag. Others cut it off at the elevator, realizing that the brand has flourished before and will continue to flourish after their tenure.

I realize we've alluded to only two sorts of account people, bright likable you and the troglodyte. There's a generous selection filling in the middle. To name a few:

• *THE COURIER.*   A sort of high-priced Federal Express. His paragraphs frequently begin with "The client said" or "Management wants." He feels that by implementing the wishes of his betters he will thereby impress his betters and advance his career. The Courier is greatly favored by troglodytes but by nobody else.

• *THE CREDIT TAKER.*   It matters nothing what the situation might be—a new business presentation, a strategy session, a media decision, even taking a vacation or going to lunch; his considerations distill down to one question: How is this going to make me look? Don't count on him for arduous toil on a difficult project if no fame is to be gained. He'll be ill that day. His efforts are applied toward prospecting that lucrative opportunity that gains the agency a headline, his name figuring prominently in the text. He'll work like the devil ignited on that one. Look for a CT in more than one corner office.

• *THE MIDNIGHT OILER.*   Yin to the Credit Taker's yang. Who performs the arduous toil on that difficult project that the CT ducked? The MO. He has it all—the brains, the integrity, the loyalty, the perseverance, midnights and Sundays too. Everything but the one that the CT makes a career of—political savvy. His facts are correct but presented too bluntly and that peeves the power player. He works his weekends on a doomed project and gets himself praised but tainted. "When will they ever learn?" the song asks. The answer is, "Too late."

And what shall we call you? How about the Creative Account Manager. It fits. You were in perfect position to field those questions from Diane and Lloyd because you knew what they were going to ask. Imagine if you hadn't known, hadn't anticipated the questions and had the answers ready. There would have been so much doubt hanging like a low fog in that room, about the value of clerics in advertising and the criticism of the church and the time required to develop a symbol, that we might easily have lost the sale.

• • •

There are always so many unruly variables that you cannot manage an account by the book. Lose a meeting, lose a campaign, lose your colleagues' confidence, lose a sharepoint, lose an account, lose a job. It happens, and it happens every day. But not to you. You're two moves ahead of the action. You have a solution and a backup solution before anyone else realizes there's a problem, and it might just be a solution no one else has tried before. That is creative account management and there's none better at it than yourself.

Well, then. Does all this seem the life you'd like to lead? Maybe account work is your line indeed.

Next question: How do you rush that line?

There are several right answers to it, considering where you are in school and how good your grades are, but also considering where your school is and how good your classes are. To explain:

In the shade of every elm on campus, professors teach: geology, theology, biology, French. They are experts in their subjects, often authorities, sometimes legends. The system insists they achieve expertise and rewards them with honors and checks. Research, discover, publish, teach. That is the system. An archaeologist teaches two semesters, then resumes exhuming Troy. So it is in all ologies save business-ology. The marketing credentials of marketing professors vary wildly from untainted academicians to former company presidents. As they vary, so does your instruction. This is not to say, hear me clearly, that your instruction is poor. It may be inspired. But it does vary school by school, and agency hirers know that.

What is true of marketing courses is doubly true of advertising courses. All too often, a student interested in advertising is caught in the twin crabclaws of circumstance. Claw One is the minimal expertise of available teachers. What advertising expert would leave the business to teach what he can earn four times the salary practicing? A very dedicated, very rare one. And even supposing one were willing, what university would have him? This is Claw Two, the impossibility of academic standards. I quote to you from the ad page of *Ad Age.*

The University of Colorado School of Journalism and Mass Communication is seeking an assistant or associate professor of advertising. Qualifications: PhD . . .

After 31 years at four agencies in this business, I am still looking forward to meeting my first PhD.

Such as it is, advertising instruction varies wildly, from the brilliant program at Boston University to irrelevant and misleading courses taught by loaner instructors from journalism. Agency hirers are keenly cognizant of the situation and in many instances prescribe against advertising courses. Here's my prescription for successful job hunting in account work.

If you're majoring in business, continue, but widen the scope of your preparation. Take a writing course. Take TV production. Join campus organizations and run for office. Keep your grades way up. If your GPA is south of 3, consider alternate futures. Show some entrepreneurial endeavor on or off campus. A gig as assistant store manager over a summer looks good on the résumé. Unless your school offers an exceptional advertising course, don't take it. You'll have to judge for yourself if it's exceptional. Check it out in the catalogue. Ask former students. What are the teacher's credentials? A class of step-by-step maxims is worse than useless. It's malpractice.

If you're majoring in liberal arts, continue, but include some business courses. Marketing, economics, computers, they're good for you and they look good. Same advice on grades and activities and advertising courses. Realize that at least as many hot prospect BAs as BBAs are being sought by agencies today.

If you're majoring in something else, consider switching to business or liberal arts. Not to say there aren't premed or music majors practicing the marketing art. There are, but those two are the high roads in.

If you're graduating, do *not* go directly to grad school. If you have the kind of credentials we've talked about, they'll get you a job. Take it. Work in the business for a couple of years. Then, if you feel a master's would be advantageous to your career, and at certain agencies in certain businesses it might be, go on to grad school. That way you'll have the experience to ground your theories in.

Caution: Not all grad schools receive good grades from agency hirers. There is a preferred list, and if your school isn't on it, you're probably wasting your time going there. The preferred list is short, only two dozen or so. If that seems elitist, even cruel, it probably is, but it's also practical. An agency's account-management personnel person will receive 5000 résumés this year. She or he can physically deal with only a fraction of them, hence the need for the list. Each agency has one, but you'll see the same prestigious schools on all of them. Here's a fairly complete New York pan-agency preferred list:

Amos Tuck	Fuqua	University of	UCLA
Columbia	Harvard	Michigan	Vanderbilt
Cornell	Michigan	Stanford	Wharton
Darden	State	Tulane	Yale

The Atlanta agency list might subtract one or two and add Georgia schools. Likewise for Chicago, Los Angeles, Dallas agencies.

The hottest of prospects, then, for account-management positions is an MBA from a preferred school with deluxe credentials including two years' agency experience.

Next in heat is a first-rate BBA or BA in liberal arts with excellent grades and activities. An MBA with no experience is no more desirable than these and has misused two years.

Start your job campaign in the fall of your senior year. Consult the agency red book at your library for the names of account-management directors or personnel directors at agencies within reach. Say you're visiting the area over vacation and you'd like to speak with someone at the agency. This letter is vitally important to you. Realize as you're writing it the effect it's going to create. Do some research on each agency. What accounts does it have? How many employees? What's the CEO's name? Sound as if you're familiar with the agency's work by *being* familiar with the agency's work. Check *Ad Age* and *Adweek*. Make your letter a compelling, witty advertisement for yourself.

Visit as many agencies as will have you. Make your interview an even better selling tool for yourself than your letter. Be wonderful. You're casing them as they're casing you. In the spring, contact your favorites again and let them know you'll be available soon. If they're interested, they'll call you in for another, higher interview and maybe an offer.

If you score, but not with the shop you were hoping for, don't fret. The important thing is that you're in. You're actually working at a real agency, and it looks mighty good on your résumé that you got that first job right out of school.

If you don't score on round one, use it as a practice round. Widen your circle and improve your technique. If the goods are there, you'll get a job.

Now, we—excuse me? You say account work sounds interesting but you'd like to investigate research and media? No sooner said than

6

RESEARCH

_R_emember when you and I determined to pitch the Rowan business? We sat staring at a vast lack of information.

How many office-furniture makers are there?
How many of them advertise?
How does Rowan furniture compare in quality and price?
Has Rowan been telling the right story in its advertising?

How do office workers rate the different makers of furniture?
How do they feel about Rowan products?
To what extent do office workers influence their companies' purchases?

All this knowledge was vital for us to make our case. Gathering facts to construct a strategy has often been compared to police work, and the comparison is valid. In both instances you scour the area for clues and follow the clues as far as they lead. Every minimal fact is important—the one you're missing might be the one that turns the case around. The police simile carries through the fact-gathering phase but not on into the ad creation. All of justice's facts add up to the fact of guilt or innocence and it ends there. The creative process only begins with an airtight strategy. It's then you reach for inspiration, into those arcane corners that have catered to the trades of poets, lovers, and televised evangelists.

Remember too that we hired a researcher to help us make our Rowan case. That is exactly what every agency, to a greater or much greater extent, does. An agency research department might be one person who brokers out projects to research services or it might be a hundred persons capable of providing almost any information the marketeers or creatives or clients might require. The size of the department is usually corollary to the size of the agency, but not always. Some midsize places are vain about their vast fact-gathering forces, and some big agencies engage only small staffs, contracting most of the work out. They view research facilities the way some women view men: They know they need one but not necessarily in the house.

Either way, there is constantly a lot of research work to be done. What do consumers think about the product? Is there room in the category for a new entry? Which model do people prefer? What flavor? Should we upgrade to an extra-strength formula? Is the current copy working? Will the new copy generate new interest?

If a photographer was to shoot a group portrait of a big agency, big-research department, he'd have to hire an ample hall. A mall movie theater would do it, just. There in the first row we'd see several well-barbered men and women smiling professionally. The account research directors. Behind them we'd see the nearly as professional assistant ARDs and behind them, platoons of market information service people and research and development people, faces and faces that the rest of us in the agency would not recognize.

We know the first-row faces well, though. ARDs are people the rest of us in the agency work with frequently, and admire. A good ARD combines two diverse skills—the resourcefulness of a detective and the salesmanship of a defense attorney. What do consumers think about the product? The ARD will propose a means of finding out. It might be a technique like PROBE, developed by one of the bigs. The PROBE researcher sits with the subject and displays photographs or drawings, meaning to elicit product attitudes. Let's say the subject is a woman and the category is cars. The researcher lays out a dozen photographs clipped from magazines and invites her to select some that illustrate how she feels about cars. She chooses a photo of a family picnic, one of grandparents, one of a house being built, one of a school bus. She's asked why she picked those pictures. "Well," she says, "we use our car for family outings and visiting, my husband uses it to buy building materials, and I drive the kids to school." Then she's shown photos of 10 autos and asked to select two she might prefer as their next car. She chooses the Chevrolet and the Dodge. Conclusion: Chevy and Dodge buyers are looking for reliable utilitarian vehicles. Or, buyers of reliable utilitarian vehicles are inclined toward Dodges and Chevrolets.

Or perhaps the subject is a man and the category is beer. He's shown photos of eight people—maybe a dock worker, a race-car driver, a diplomat, a businessman, an oil rigger, a football player, a farmer, and a college student. Then he's shown a list of four beers: Bud Light, Heineken, Amstel, and Schlitz. Question: If these were people, which would they be? Note that the question is not which people drink which beers. That would merely summon up the characters seen in those beers' commercials. Which people would those beers be elicits the subject's feelings about the beer itself. "Okay," he says, "Bud Light is the college student, Heineken is the businessman, Amstel is the diplomat, and Schlitz is the dock worker." Why? "Well, Bud Light because I think of it as young and smart. Heineken because it's very good but expensive, Amstel because it's imported and hard to find, and Schlitz because it's worker beer, honky-tonk beer."

One man's attitude, yes, but when it's endorsed by most of the men in a session, some conclusive insights can be drawn. PROBE research and its several counterparts produce small but intense samples of feelings and attitudes that never would have been brought to light by broader but shallower techniques.

Whatever technique the ARD suggests, it might not be what the client has in mind. Sometimes a client will admit the need for research but suggest an antiseptic little study that will do little more than confirm the current strategy. Here's where the salesmanship comes in. More probing (and more expensive) research might turn up disturbing evidence that the current strategy is headed for distress. Which could lead to criticism of or even sacking of the current strategists. The ARD needs to sell the probing research to the people it could discomfit.

Then there's the research that discomfits creative folks—commercial testing. It's like this: You conceive a campaign for Tide and you think it's awesome. The client thinks it's awesome. But will the people think it's awesome? If they do, if your test spot tests favorably, your campaign will go on to full production and television airing. If they don't, if the test response is negative, your allegedly awesome campaign will join the million others in the Death-by-Testing Mausoleum.

Go on to full production? That is correct. Your 30-second spot will not be fully produced for testing. Full production these days averages about $125,000 per spot, so naturally no client company can afford to full-produce all the dozens, even hundreds, of test commercials it needs. Test spots are made in one-half the time for one-tenth the cost of the real thing, using techniques like half-inch videotape and 8mm film. Which is only realistic, but it doesn't ease your worry over those color nuances or special effects that can't be done for the money. And that's only one of your worries. Another is the test method itself. There are about a dozen techniques for testing commercials, all with advantages, all with flaws. Let's start with the audience. Who are those people who will or won't think it's awesome? They aren't everybody. A researcher researching research companies reports that 38% of the people who are asked to participate in a survey or study say no. What's different about the other 62%? Are they more dutiful? More friendly? More opinionated? More idle? Whatever they are, they're your jury.

Now the methods. The one we've passed or failed by for years is called Standard Burke Day-After. Burke inserts your test spot into a prime-time television program, then the next day telephones at random until it locates 200 people who were watching the show at the moment it faded to your commercial. The call goes like this:

> *Hello, Mrs. Mangiacavallo? Burke Testing calling. Did you watch* Hill Street Blues *last night?*
> *Yes, I did.*
> *Were you watching when Belker bit the rabbi?*
> *Yes, I was.*
> *Do you recall seeing a detergent commercial?*
> *Um, let me see. . . . Yes, Tide.*
> *Can you recall what it said? What points did it make? What did it show?*

When Mrs. Mangiacavallo mentioned Tide, that response was noted under Unaided Recall. If she hadn't, the interviewer would have prompted her with the brand name. If she'd responded yes to that, an X would have been entered under Aided Recall. Which is good but not as good as Unaided. Now Mrs. M. must prove she saw the spot by alluding to some feature of it, preferably something not generic to all Tide commercials. This is the prickly part. Maybe the good lady is ill or tired or busy or distracted. The dog's eating the cat's food. She can't think to remember. Or maybe, just as your spot came on last night, her husband came home with Chinese food. She saw Belker but not the spot, but she counts. Well, the Burke folks say, that's possible, but remember we're doing this in three cities with 200 certified viewers each. Certified *program* viewers, you say, only about 160 commercial viewers and only about 35 related recallers. A swing of five either way passes or fails your awesome spot. Maybe, they say, but over the years the peaks and valleys even out.

Right. Just hope you're a peak this time.

The random selection of Burke is its power and its flaw. There is no more real-world technique, and for that reason it's still the most widely employed testing method in the business. But it's impossible to analyze the audience or the persuasiveness of the advertising. You don't know how rich, poor, young, or old Mrs. Mangiacavallo is, or what effect the spot had on her opinion of Tide. All Burke truly measures is the ad's intrusiveness, and even *that* is suspect. Say Mrs. M. responds, "I saw a lady pouring Tide from an orange box." Yes, that occurred in your spot, but it's occurred in every Tide spot ever made. Should her response count? Years ago it wouldn't have, but now, with viewers harder to come by and verbatims growing ever feebler, it probably would.

What is a good Burke score? Depends on the product category, but for detergents you'll take a 25. That means 75% of the people who saw Belker bite the rabbi, and so presumably saw your spot, couldn't remember it the next day. And that's good! In fact, if you cull out the wussy responses like "pouring from an orange box," your real score is more like 15.

For all these reasons, Burke is losing ARD recommendations to more controllable and analytic methods.

Like ARS. A hundred people are invited to a theater to preview a new TV pilot. Three test commercials are inserted at the breaks. Then a second pilot is shown, containing three more test spots. The viewers answer some questions about the shows, then answer some more about which products they prefer in the test categories. As they entered the theater, they selected a number of items they'd like to receive as door prizes. Now, as they're leaving the theater, after exposure to the advertising, they select again. The difference between pre- and post-exposure brand choice is assumed to be a measure of the advertising's persuasiveness. Mm-hm.

Three days later, about half of them are telephoned and asked to recall the commercials, with much the same line of questioning as Burke's. Responses are then correlated to the usage information and the door prize selections, and a report is prepared for the agency.

Advantages? Audience segmentation: ARS separates the rich from the poor by address selection, then infiltrates some personal information into the pilot questionnaire. Intrusiveness: If you can remember a commercial three days later, it's intrusive. Persuasiveness: If they chose Cheer coming in and Tide going out, what else did it but your spot?

Problems? The herd reaction: In any group research project, individuals are likely to be swayed by mass reaction or by neighbor reaction ("Which one did you choose?"). Door prize persuasion: It limits the test entries (Ford's not going to give away an Escort), and value is a corrupting factor. Obviously you'll take the expensive stuff even if you hated the spots.

ARS is recommended only in cases where intrusiveness is the prime criterion.

Then there's ASI Recall Plus. Two hundred people are invited to view a test program on a cable TV channel. Next day they're telephoned and given the usual line of questioning. But. Here's the new wrinkle. Now they're asked to turn on their cable sets and switch to an unused channel where they watch the test commercial *again*. They're asked comprehension questions, persuasion questions, diagnostic questions, and demographic questions.

Advantages? Intrusiveness: about the same as Burke. Comprehension: You've got the respondent on the phone, so ask away—copy points, main message, visual recall. Same with persuasion and diagnostics. Problems? Almost none.

ASI Recall Plus may be the copy-testing system of the future. It is highly recommended for almost all occasions.

The ARD has more testing tools than an alchemist, too many to describe in detail, but there is one more that wants mention. Focused groups. Ten people sit around a table and discuss your subject, guided by a moderator. What subject? Anything you need. Fast cars, Maalox, dieting, ocean cruises, orange juice, church attendance, or Maxi-Pads.

The ARD will engage the service of a focused-group facility (there are thousands), which include a wired room, an adjacent client room that looks into the wired room through a one-way glass, food, and the 10 participants. Fast cars? Ten speeders. Maalox? Ten tummyachers. Dieting? Ten fatties. You ask, they find, at $40 a head. The ARD can run the session personally or hire a moderator. The group will rap about your topic for two hours while you watch and take notes and prompt the moderator on the secret one-way ear radio.

What you learn from 10 people is, of course, not projectable nationally, but it can be a good indication. Will people believe a diet candy can work? Would they prefer a different flavor Maalox? Would they accept a performance car from Korea? Focused groups can ease away client fears about a strategy or a line, or they can surface problems early, when they're cheaper to solve.

All of the above show why a good ARD is indispensable to the advertising process.

Indispensable to the ARD are those latter-row platoons of fact gatherers and vote counters. Daily they sit in the lime-jello light of their computer screens, entering and retrieving facts, or before alps of questionnaires, sorting stacks of yes and no.

Research services these days, in house and out, are developing tremendous data bases. Billions of facts are being programmed onto floppy disks concerning everything remotely relevant to the business. Not only test scores but consumer-preference trends and behavioral studies that are generated, purchased and pirated from any and every source.

Who are these fact people, why are they fact people, and how did they get to be? Their backgrounds are as varied as foreign legionnaires'. Their degrees comprise many combinations of two and three letters signifying every major in the catalogue. A most common designator is personality. Many, though not all, seem pleased to sit for hours alone with data and don't mind if they never get to meet an account executive.

Their pay is middling and their hours lonely, but if fact gathering sounds like something you'd like to do, credentials in statistics and computers are essential.

Agencies, in fact, are minor players in the research business. The client corporations engage far more research people. But by far the greatest seeker of research talent is the independent research industry. There are 1500 firms listed in the catalogue of suppliers, ranging from huge services like Yankelovich and Roper to the local one-on-one interview shops.

Research is an industry that can't help but grow, both in size and capability. More and more products are competing for the same people's dollars, votes, viewing hours. Accurate measurement of success or failure becomes more and more vital as competition tightens.

These days, as you read this, research in all of its applications is passing through a period of considerable change. It has already become a far more accurate tool of measure than it ever has been before. One large reason for the change is that little box of bars you find on your box of corn flakes. Remember those bygone days a few years ago, when the supermarket check-out clerk would bottom-up your groceries to read the prices? No more. Now in most markets she slides them across the scanner and the electronic eye reads the prices.

These days a lot more than price is being programmed into those mystery lines. Brand, size, flavor, color, model, store name, and location, all these and more are being factored into the wee jailhouse window by store chains in participation with market research firms. That information is then harvested nationwide, tallied, and collated by the researchers and set up on the desks of client brand managers every Monday morning. Imagine this now. A brand manager arrives on Monday to find a stack of facts next to his morning coffee: his sales of the week nationwide, by size, flavor, store, etc., *and* his competitors' sales.

That's not the way it used to be, not so long ago. It used to be that a brand manager would attend a research report session every two months, given by a market research company. Compiling and analyzing the data was a lengthy task then, so the information was always stale. Sales reports for June and July, for instance, would not be ready for presentation until August. The delay was irksome, like reading week-old baseball scores on vacation, but sometimes it was worse than that. Sometimes it was calamitous. By the time the brand got the bad news, it could be too late to do much about it. And the news they got was little more than brand, size, and type of store. The eight-ounce Pepto-Bismol is off 5% in major drug chains, that sort of thing.

Now the good news is that the brand manager receives 10 times as many facts, once a week. The bad news is, those facts arrive unsorted. He needs to pick the pertinent needles out of the stack. The better/ worse news is that the market research industry now has the data-gathering ability to increase that stack of facts 10 times. Research vendors are now segmenting information by region, by city, even by neighborhood. One company now offers a data base that dices the country into 240,000 neighborhoods of 340 households each. Our brand manager may now order weekly sales reports on his own and competitors' brands by price, size, color, flavor, model, and store, cross-referenced by a quarter-million neighborhoods. Now that, folks, is a stack.

Obviously, priority one is a data-processing technique that will cull out desired data, and I'm sure we'll have it shortly. But consider now the implications of this data breakdown by neighborhood. One re-searcher sitting at a computer can tap you out a perfect portrait of any area in the country of any size, from state to street corner. How? Easy. She punches in bar code data for telltale items—baby food, wine, acne cream, pet food, TV dinners, denture adhesive, and espresso coffee—then correlates those with car sales and magazine subscriptions, and she can tell you everything you want to know about a neighborhood. She'll give you the relative index of singles, babies, golden-agers, teens, and young marrieds and tell you how rich or poor they all are. What's that you're selling? Pampers? She'll print you out a list of the 25 most affluent high-baby-index towns in the land. Fasteeth? The 25 top golden-ager markets.

Now consider the implications of all *that*.

Used to be, media decisions were based on cost per thousand, presuming the vehicle would search out the prospect. Achieving desired cost per thousand meant, of course, using national media. Only by buying network television or national magazines could the necessary millions of prospective customers be reached. The only question then was, which shows and which books? The answers were relatively ob-vious. If you're Reebok, runners' magazines; if you're Mr. Clean, *Good Housekeeping* and daytime television.

But. Now factor in the new abilities and see how they scramble the old assumptions. Let's say you're Pampers. Up till now you'd have used new-mother magazines like *Parents,* plus daytime TV. Why? Cost per thousand. Only national media can pull in the millions necessary to an efficient cost per thousand. But let's talk about that thousand. How many of a thousand watchers of *All My Children* are new mothers or pregnant or even thinking about getting pregnant soon? A hundred? Not even. That is a 90% waste rate, and that's considered good! At least it has been until now. Now you ask your researcher for the 25 top affluent baby markets and you make new media decisions! Maybe you cut your national budget by a third and allocate that money for the top 25. Not states, not cities, *neighborhoods.* How do you reach neighborhoods? Cable TV, newspapers, radio, direct mail, outdoor, point of sale.

There's a story about two scientists that I've always found relevant to advertising. One is a theoretical scientist and the other is an applied scientist, and they're arguing this hypothesis: A man approaches the woman he loves and with each step he cuts the distance between them by half. "Well of course," the theoretical scientist says, "he'll never reach her." "True," replies the applied scientist, "but he'll get close enough."

Advertising, for all these years since Lyman Morse cashed his first commission check, has been a business of "close enough." Especially advertising research. Test scores, consumer trends, awareness, attitudes, prospect-to-people ratios, the importance of pricing, flavor, brand name. There are numbers for all but they're all approximations. The country is so vast, testing methods are so inexact, you take your best shot, and close enough is good enough.

New research abilities are already narrowing the gap between approximation and verifiable fact. Advertising research may never get to be an exact science, but it may one day soon get close enough.

There's no question that research is undergoing more change faster than any other area of advertising. Some agency research departments are now being assigned to do the strategic detective work that creative and account folks used to do. To explain: Every time a new campaign is needed, the first process in the development of that campaign is thorough detective work. You compose a market target and zero in on the bulls-eye, that sector of consumerdom most likely to buy your product. Within that bulls-eye there are buyers and nonbuyers. Why are the buyers buying and the nonbuyers not buying? The available information, *all* the available information, needs to be sifted in search of a critical insight. Then that insight becomes the central thought of the new campaign. This process, first the sifting then the creating, is the task of what I call the Artful Detective. Full disclosure of the A.D. and his M.O. will follow in the chapter on creativity, but let's assign him to a test case just to show you what I mean about that critical insight.

Test case: Campbell's Soup. For years, Campbell's advertising strategy read something like this: To convince people, especially mothers, that Campbell's offers a variety of good-tasting soups that are convenient for serving any time.

Remember the tune?

> *Mm-mm good*
> *Mm-mm good*
> *That's what Campbell's Soups are,*
> *Mm-mm good.*

Somewhere along the way, Campbell's realized that although everyone in the country knew their soups were mm-mm good, the campaign was no longer moving cans. Sales were mm-mm sluggish. What to do? Call in (sound the *Dragnet* notes) the Artful Detective.

Campbell's had huge data-bank accounts, thousands of numbers and facts. Sales reports, consumer-habit studies, focused-group discussions, TV commercial test analyses, all needed to be examined and cross-checked. As the A.D. sifted, conclusions emerged. Life-styles were changing. There were fewer kids and more lunch options, like school programs and Burger King. Campbell's is one of the nation's largest grocery store franchises. Every market from Grand Union to Pop's on the corner has a shelf full of red-and-white cans. Availability was not the problem.

The problem was that *Mom* had a shelf full of red-and-white cans and she wasn't opening them. Why not? Because she didn't really consider canned soup to be real food. Sickbed food, bachelor food, quick-fix lunch food, but not *real* food.

Of course it *is* real food, in that it's quite nourishing, far better for you than a burger, fries, and a Coke. But too many women didn't think of it that way. There's the critical insight. It first becomes the central thought of the new strategy:

To convince people, especially mothers, that Campbell's soups are wholesome and nourishing as well as good-tasting. Something like that. Then the critical insight becomes the central thought of the new campaign, and here's where the Artful Detective calls on his artful part. He creates selling magic around the thought. You've heard the results:

Campbell's . . . soup is good food.

Case closed. Another job well done by (*Dragnet* notes) the Artful Detective.

One more example of critical insight before we return to research's new role. Nearly 60% of American women work outside the home. About half of them work in offices, and most of *them* dress in proper business attire. Quite properly so. They mean to minimize the differences between themselves and their male colleagues down to intelligence and ability, so they dress very much like their male colleagues, in pinstripe suit, white blouse, maroon scarf or jabot. But. *Underneath* all that neuterality, two-thirds of those women wear erotic lingerie! So reports a survey done by Woolite. It's the businesswoman's way of saying, "I can think with any man, I can even dress with any man, but when you get right down to it, Jack, I'm a WOMAN!" Consider how critical that insight is to such as Maidenform and Hanes, as well as to Woolite.

My Artful Detective is, as you've surmised, a copywriter. Or an art director. Sometimes an account person. Sometimes a team. In the new scheme of things, though, much of the detecting will be performed by the research person. All of that information the A.D. sifted through was, after all, research. Why couldn't the research people have run it all through their computer and come to the same conclusion sooner? The answer is, simply, up until now it hasn't been their job.

From now on, at certain agencies anyway, it will be. (Although, if you'll permit a clearly biased editorial comment, I'll believe it when I see it.)

Entry level for the front-row position is assistant ARD. Essential credentials would be a degree in behavioral science or statistics, including many credits of math and psych, with a heavy overlay of marketing.

If your curiosity starts you wondering why people spend, vote, and view as they do, maybe research is your industry. The good ones are always that way—curious, wondering why. Get a taste of the job after school or between semesters. Research companies are eternally looking for field interviewers. Try some selling too—brushes, pots, cosmetics door to door, learn first hand why people spend or don't spend. Selling pots on television isn't vastly different from selling them on the porch. If you like the taste of research, steer your major toward that front-row seat.

7

MEDIA

*B*ack at the beginning, as we mentioned back at the beginning, advertising agents were media middlemen. Lyman D. Morse called on merchants, persuading them that advertising meant higher sales. He brought along sample books of competitors' ads to press the point. For every ad sold, newspapers and magazines paid Lyman D. a commission of 15%.

After a time, prospective customers began inquiring how they could be provided with copy and layout even snappier than the competitors'.

So the media reps hired copywriters, and that's how the creative department came to be. Then the reps ceased selling space for publications and began buying space for client businesses, and that's how the industry came to be. The new agencies opened downtown offices with their names on wavy glass doors. N.W. Ayer Advertising. J. Walter Thompson Advertising. In those days using your first initial was considered dignified. Nowadays they'd be Nat Ayer and Jim Thompson. They spent their days contacting clients while their copywriters stayed in the office and wrote copy. Those first account executives were called contact men back then. They were still called contact men in the late '50s when I started at Young and Rubicam.

The second wave of agencies, in the early years of this century, opened as partnerships, contact and copy. Young and Rubicam, Benton & Bowles. You and I. One of the first things they did, as you and I did, was to hire someone to do the space buying while they went about contacting and copywriting. And that's how the media department came to be.

These days media departments are segmented into planning and buying specialties. They apportion budgets of multiple millions into several of dozens of media. Just think of where you've ever seen an ad. Not only on those TV and radio stations, in all those magazines and papers, but on matchbooks and billboards, airport walls and taxi roofs, on plane banners and bus rumps. With those multiple millions, media people decide which TV shows get sponsored and which don't, and therefore which you watch. And yet, essentially what they're doing is no more than what Ayer and Thompson were doing a hundred years ago: getting their clients' messages in front of the right people for the right price.

PLANNING IT

And who are those right people? How do you apportion the clients' budget to reach the goodliest number of them the ideal number of times? If answering these questions is your job, then you are called a media planner.

Media planning has been called a colossal board game you play with somebody else's money. You bet that money on media options. Hundreds of thousands of option permutations. Think of all those magazines on all those newsstands all over the country, weekly and monthly, and all those newspapers next to them, weekly and daily. Think of all those radio stations in all those towns, all those programs around the clock. Think of all those TV programs on all those TV stations, network and independent. They're all for sale.

One good thing is that you almost can't be wrong. At least no one can point the finger at you if sales slip. After all, all you did was play the numbers the computer printed. Then again, you can hardly take a bow if sales rise, if all you did was play the computer numbers.

But is that all you'd do, play the numbers? Or would you use some reason and sense and some intuition and play some numbers that aren't on the screen? A true story:

The product was an acne cream and the market target was clearly defined—boys and girls 12 to 17. Media planning always begins with the market target and rarely is it clearly defined. Think of it. Who's the target for Bufferin? Any adult with a headache. For Alka-Seltzer? Any adult with a headache and/or stomachache. How about Jell-O? Sony TV? Band-Aids? The answer is most everybody, and that's what's wrong with the answer. There's no efficient way to reach most everybody. You can try cutting them out of the pack—catching rock fans with headaches in *Rolling Stone* and Presbyterians with headaches in *Presbyterian Life*, but the usual method is to go for the big shows most everybody watches.

Not so with acne cream. The target stands out in sharp relief—boys and girls, 12 to 17. You know zits don't quit at 17, so why break off the category there? Two reasons. One, the heaviest onset occurs during these six years and two, teenage media concentrates there. The computer said, to reach the goodliest number of teens at the right price, use magazines and MTV. The agency had prepared some magazine ads that looked good and tested well. Case closed? Not quite. The media planner was uneasy with the plan. He ran the numbers again. Reach, frequency, cost, all admirable. But look at the magazines—whom were they reaching? *Glamour, Seventeen,* they were reaching girls. The list was biased but zits aren't. Well, the computer said, boys don't buy magazines. Then why be in magazines, why not radio? A second argument: The product's image was a little dated, and that's something radio can correct. There is no medium as today as radio. Teen radio is all today. To a 16-year-old, two years ago is "before my time." Never mind the creative department's howls that they had dandy print and no radio copy. Never mind the client's dismay at sidestepping the computer. The planner carried the day because he did something the computer can't do: He thought.

Do you think you might like that job?

Breaking into media is a little less difficult than breaking into copywriting, which is only a little less difficult than breaking into the Kremlin. The most plentiful degree among planners is a BA, in any of a variety of majors. But the most plentiful characteristic is a significant degree of smarts. A good résumé with a better letter will probably get you an interview. The interviewer will be probing for thinking, especially strategic thinking ability. As one media director said, "If I think an applicant is manipulating me, I hire him."

Flushed with success, you begin work, at likely the single most miserable job in the business. An assistant planner works two-shift days for pitiable pay, learning all day and grunt-laboring into the night. At ten o'clock in the evening, the agency's lights shine only upon cleaning crews and assistant media planners. Your indentured servitude lasts from six months to a year when you move to the planner level and bequeath your No-Doz to a fresh new assistant.

If media looks worth looking into, look first at some trade magazines. *Advertising Age* and *Media Decisions* will give you a clearer idea of what the career is like. If you're still in school, you'll need to do some self-guidance. There are no degrees in media, you can't major in it, but you can prepare. Take some marketing courses to get familiar with the business in general. Take a computer course—it's a tool you'll be using. Above all, learn the methods of strategy. Take classes in selling strategy, economic, even military, strategy. The ability to lay out a course of action and to set up the sequence steps is fundamental to a planner.

Do some selling on the side. Witness firsthand why people buy or don't buy.

When you're ready, consult an agency directory. Write for interviews to the directors of media. Remember that your letter is your advertisement. The director doesn't care if you play water polo. He or she wants to know that you understand media and why you think you'll be good at it. Build your letter around your principal personal selling point.

BUYING IT

If you pay the retail price for your clothes, says the maxim, you'll never be a media buyer. Media buyers are world-class hagglers, and the better they haggle the richer they get. The very good ones retire young.

A very good media buyer will be up to 50 percent more efficient than a not very good one. He or she will purchase a third more airtime for the same dollars for the agency and its client. That differential requires the use of several zeroes and commas to compute, and that can make an agency very appreciative.

Now hold it, you demur, how is this possible? A latitude of buying efficiency implies a latitude of price. Aren't there fixed costs for airtime?

In a word, no. Everything is negotiable. Broadcast time, radio and television, is, all of it, one big flea market. To illustrate, imagine an afternoon talk show on a minor channel. The *Portly Short Show,* rated at about a 3. Book value for one 30-second spot, $600. Two telephone conversations, each leading to the purchase of four spots.

ONE

SELLER: Channel nine sales.

BUYER: This is Nick from Nick's Dodge World on the highway. You know, I really like that *Portly Short Show.* He's always ready with a joke, and he has fabulous guests. Do you think I could buy a couple of spots on that show? What does a spot run?

SELLER: That show fills up fast. Goes for $750 a shot.

BUYER: $750 . . . oh . . . That's a little steep. . . .

SELLER: Tell you what. We like to treat our first-time customers right. I'll give you two for, let's see, $1400. Wait. Maybe I can do better. Can you go four? I'll try to swing this upstairs. Four for $2500. Save you $500.

BUYER: Wow. If you can swing it, I'll take it. Thanks.

TWO

SELLER: Channel nine sales.

BUYER: What've you got for me cheap? I've got a good offer at channel five. They're waiting for an answer. What about that dog of a talk show with that fat mutt, what's his name?

SELLER: Portly Short?

BUYER: Got to be the dullest hour on television. Give me a price on four.

SELLER: Four bills each?

BUYER: Three and a half. Think it over, but think fast.

SELLER: Don't have to. You got it.

Buyer One paid $625, Buyer Two paid $350 for exactly the same 30 seconds. Why? Supply and demand? Yes. Buyer One evinced too high a demand. Bad haggling. He paid for it. Manipulation? Yes. Buyer Two waited till just before closing and then pressured the seller. Good haggling. He profited.

Does this sort of pushcart transacting carry beyond *Portly Short* to network megabuys? You bet, and when you multiply the money by millions you can appreciate the agency's appreciation of a Buyer Two.

Large corporations often select one of their several advertising agencies to be what's called the media agency of record. All of the company's media money for, let's say, prime-time television will be consigned to the agency of record. That money empowers that agency's buyer with a buyer's wieldiest weapon—clout. So armed, he strides through NBC, CBS, ABC, and the independents selecting and rejecting. He screens the fall programming prospects, buying into this one but not into that one.

He'll take that dog off their hands if they'll throw in eight Monday night movies and a Superbowl preview. He thus outlays $40 million and influences what a nation will watch on television in the age-old manner of a Sicilian housewife buying a flounder.

A media buyer plays a board game too, but unlike the planner, he (and everyone else) soon knows whether he won or lost and how big. Did that show he selected become a hit? Did the one he rejected flop? If so, he's king for a week. If not, if the hit flopped and the flop hit, he's slug of the month and he won't be the buyer next year and maybe neither will his agency.

That's what the business of buying media is like. Interested? You begin as a network assistant doing logging and other paperwork, making sure, in essence, that the right spot gets played at the right time. From there it's buying assistant. You deal for small stuff like spot radio. Then you're a buyer, with client responsibility. Step four is buying supervisor, and here's where you start to make money. As associate director, next, you're earning stockbroker money and from there on there's no limit, only skill and circumstance.

And that's only on the agency side. There are hundreds of media buying services, chiefed frequently by former agency kings of the week. And that's only on the buying side. Think of the selling side. All those stations and magazines employ salespeople like the *Portly Short* seller who made a big bundle on Buyer One and a small bundle—but better than no bundle—on Buyer Two.

Sitting there reading this, you already know if you'd be good at buying media. You can't really study for the field, but you can train for it. Take a booth in a flea market and sharpen your haggle. Then open that agency registry and write those media directors. Again, your letter is your personal ad.

8

CREATION

*W*ell, I might have known. You're impressed with the importance of account work, then again media has its fascinating aspects, and research might be the most interesting of all. And yet, like Circe the enchantress calling Ulysses to her silvery sheets, creative beckons to you. You know it's the least defined, least permanent position in a vague and perilous profession, yet you must drop anchor and see for yourself. Then so you will.

Least defined, it is all of that. This job of advertising creative person is, maybe more than any other in modern business, what you make of it. Over 30 years at four agencies I've known probably 500 writers and art directors. I've watched each of them define his or her job, and therefore life, uniquely—in response to untouchable factors like the nature of the agency, the state of its and the nation's economy, and to personal factors as well—intelligence, talent, ambition, courage, temperament, all of those and who knows, early weaning and toilet training too.

Creative job definitions range, like coffee-cake crumbs, all over the table, but let's see if we can't gather a few categories together.

• *THE CIVIL SERVANT.* Have you dealt with a government bureau? Then you know the service to be competent if indolent and only marginally civil. Our CS generates competent professional work for competent professional pay, with now and then an inspiration if the muse happens to light upon his collar (between 9 and 5 but not between 12 and 2). Why, says he, do more work than you have to, after all? You get the same paycheck either way, and some boob of an account person or client is only going to kill it anyway. Come to think twice about it, I don't see so many of the CS breed as once I did along the halls. Perhaps a fallout effect from the mergers, as we'll see later.

• *THE MISPLACED MARKETING MAJOR.* We've agreed, haven't we, that the agency marketing department is in effect the longer marketing arm of the manufacturer. And therefore that account management is the agency's main line. We have.

We have not agreed that the creative department is the longer arm of the marketing department. The MMM, however, would see it so and propose a cogent case for the rightness of his view: The business of an agency is the making and placing of a client's advertising; critical to the making and placing of a client's advertising is the keeping of the client; critical to keeping the client is keeping the client happy; clients are kept happy in diverse ways—good buddyness, constant work, good work; account folks need and deserve complete cooperation in keeping the client happy. That's where the MMM steps in. Good buddyness? Count on him for dinner or tennis. Constant work? At your service, although the weight of the work might outweigh its merit. Good work? Coming right up. Brilliant work? Mmm. That he'll have to get some help with. The MMM's business acumen often outweighs his creative talent, which doesn't mean he doesn't attain success in the creative business. Quite the contrary. If fair winds prevail and the stars are right, he can sail the perilous seas to the corner office. One such executive creative director laughingly looks back at his lack of talent as an art director. A client once asked him if, in the future, he would please label his drawn figures as either men or women. Directing work requires a different talent than doing it.

• *THE ARTFUL DETECTIVE.* Let's define the Civil Servant's imperative as serving out his time, doing the minimum work for the maximum money. Let's say that the Misplaced Marketing Major's imperative is optimum cooperation with account and client toward trouble-free maintenance of the business. The Artful Detective's then would be, first, determining the brand's most persuasive aspect and, second, creating dazzling advertising behind it. But that, young friends, is one labor-intensive imperative, many times more tiring than waiting for a muse or papering a wall with lightweight layouts. This quest for truth and brilliance can be more than fatiguing, please take heed. It is often thankless, frustrating, and as your quest sometimes leads to confrontation, dangerous. Which is why the Artful Detective's imperative has fewer perpetrators than it deserves.

It is to me, however, the only way. It's the way I propose to you. The way to conceive, create, present, and produce an advertising idea. As Fred said to Ginger, let's start with step one.

CONCEPTION

The brand's most persuasive aspect? What is there about this item that can make it seem most desirable to the largest number of people? Now and again there's a clear advantage. Tropicana Orange Juice is truly fresh-squeezed while other brands are reconstituted from concentrate. When the case is this clear, look no further. It rarely is. More often, there is an advantage but you'll need to dig to find it, as you and I did with Rowan Office Furniture. As you dig you'll hit a difference.

There's almost always some kind of difference. Is that difference an advantage? Sometimes it is but no one's noticed it yet, as with Rowan. Sometimes the difference can be developed into an advantage, but that requires thinking. And more digging. Dig into the demographics, the consumer stats. Might the difference be an advantage to a sector of the market? The most affluent or the most influential sector? Sometimes it's a difference that looks like a disadvantage, but addressed to a unique sector, it becomes a selling point. Ivory Snow is a soap. It lacks the cleaning power of detergents. Fatal disadvantage? Not when addressed to mothers of newborns who'll happily trade the power for the mildness.

More often still, dig as deep as you will, you'll find no advantage nor any gnarl of difference that can feasibly be disguised as one. In this case, your job is to create a preference for the product. Persuade people to like your brand better than its identical competitor, as we did for Friar's. It is at this point you move to step two, the creation of dazzling advertising. This is the step the CS seldom takes because it's too laborious and the MMM nearly never because he lacks the wattage.

Two notes before we step.

As you've been digging you've felt a tugging. A chance remark began it, or a quiet fact on a page. A small tug, scarcely discernible, that said Look This Way. You conversed with the account folks, checked over the stats again, read an article, and there was the tug again, harder. Look This Way. At this point, go back and chat with the account folks again. Open the thought to them, but do it subtly, as if it were no more than a passing notion. Here's what will happen. If the thought is invalid, that is, illegal or counter to policy or previously conceived, they'll spot it. If the thought is valid, best let them in on it early, but carefully. Idea mortality is highest during infancy. Conspire with them on the parentage of the thought, and you'll find them much more positively inclined at the presentation stage.

Second note on conception. On rare occasions you will come up against a thoroughbred dog, a product that is slightly to vastly inferior to competition and that should have perished with Ipana and Silvercup. When that happens I recall the old Don Adams defense-lawyer rountine. He's defending a Mrs. Glick, clearly guilty of having dispatched Mr.

Glick with a .45 revolver. In his opening remarks he says, "Gentlemen of the jury, the prosecuting attorney is lucky. He's got facts. All I've got is trickery and deceit. Well, let's see how far we can get with that."

Right, then. You've completed the hard half of the job, determining the brand's most persuasive aspect, the product point of view. Now it's time for the harder half.

IDEATING

"You know the way," the guard says. "You ought to know it by now." The stones along the corridor are coated over with ancient moss. At the end of the long shadowy walkway is The Room. The light inside shines out through the little door window, striped by the bars. The guard makes a mock bow as you enter, then closes the iron door shut and clicks home the ancient bolt. On the steel table there's a pad and four pencils. The walls are dull gray, all graffiti effaced. No distractions, not even a fly to watch. Write. Write and don't come out until it's written. Dante sat in that chair. Steinbeck did, but then so did Jacqueline Susann and Mickey Spillane. Somewhere water drips. Write. You've brought your notes, you know the point of view, write. Think. Write. No one can help you now.

Except of course your partner, whom we've been omitting from the play-by-play to make our points more clearly. But he's been there, he or she, in on every play. He's in The Room with you now, sharing your agony.

You begin with the process of reasoning out. Reason out from the point of view. If *this* is true then *that* would be true. And so would *that* and so would *that*. As you do it, make your mind a TV screen. Let whatever images that come to mind play on the screen. Come at the subject from other angles. The customers, the competition. Free associate. There are those who begin the process by running the subject through a succession of techniques—candids, a personality, slice-of-life, testimonials, how about a song? They generally achieve what their method deserves—superficial dreck that melds into the mass of superficial dreck that is 90% of commercial television. Don't do it their way. Keep coming back to the point of view and reasoning out from it. Read through the documents with your partner. Read aloud. Let those images play freely on your mind-screen. You'll work your way through a series of how abouts, projecting each one on the screen, always conscious of imposed limitations—legal, media, budget. How about, what if, suppose we, how about . . . then it happens. One of those how abouts spins your head about on its socket. Yes. Yes yes yes. You play it on the screen and it works. Yes. It's right. It fits. Yes. You play it again and it locks. Yes.

There is no moment like that moment anywhere else in this business.

A few extra words on partners. First on the he and the she of it. Most and longest-lasting partnerships I've seen have been he–he or she–she combos. Now and then a she–he partnership works well, but not often. The different views on life from opposite banks of the gender gap usually make it tougher to get together on an idea. The closer you two begin as people, the more likely you are to create well together. You'll find that the art–copy difference is difference enough.

There are those who labor alone in The Room, either by preference or by lack. By my lights though, solitary ideation seldom generates the creative product that cross-pollination can.

I wish you a partner to share your agony and ecstasy with, as gifted as several I've had, most especially my partner of 15 years, the most gifted of all, Mr. Albert Silver.

PRESENTING

You're released from The Room on your own recognizance two days later, carrying a layout for a magazine ad and a storyboard for a 30-second television commercial. You'll be presenting those, refining as you go, to:

1 Your creative director
2 The account people
3 Possibly senior account or creative directors
4 Client people
5 Possibly senior client people

Your goal of course is approval by all, with permission to produce. That will mean five shows with three distinct formats for the creative, account, and client audiences. Your process is complicated by the fact that you're presenting new thinking as well as new executions, but that can be turned to advantage. Sell them on the thinking and the ads will follow as naturally as five follows four. As you lead them through your point of view, watch their faces. Are they smiling, nodding in approval as you sink your points home like darts in the bulls-eye? Don't let the smile fade. Move smoothly to the ads, speaking glibly as you do, maintaining the rhythm of those steady nods.

If perchance they aren't smiling but frowning, or worse, staring at you as if you were dippy, and you feel your darts thudding into the wall, call time. Thrash out the idea at the point-of-view stage; never uncover the ads. You might waste an idea that could be retrieved. But let us posit a positive postulation for pragmatic purposes: Let's say they love it.

Gathering your forces for your presentation, as your audience settles into its chairs, you may feel yourself in top form. Or maybe not. Headache, hangover, stage fright, any of the many afflictions the performing flesh is heir to may be upon you at the critical moment, and your show will suffer. Over the years I've found it exceedingly useful to gather my thoughts into a think piece, one or two deft pages that not only set up the executions but accompany them through future presentations I won't attend. Remember Lloyd at Friar's, the marketing director who presented our work?

A word on the work itself, your ad and your storyboards. The word is unmistakable. Make your words and especially your pictures unmistakable—showing clearly what you intend with no room for misinterpretation, because if you don't you may be sure that someone will misinterpret, probably someone important, especially if you're not there to explain. Perfect pictures, dialogue, and video directions. Do you intend a sexy female winking seductively? Then draw one and draw her well, not a circle with curly hair and one eye closed. And make those video directions come to life: SHE FOLLOWS HIM WITH HER GAZE, WINKS

VIDEO: OPEN ON PAUL REVERE, LOOKING UPSET

AUDIO: Hi, I'm Paul Revere. I've been on the road all night...racing around, gulping coffee...

VIDEO: HE INDICATES HIS MIDSECTION

AUDIO: I had chicken pot pie for dinner. It's sitting here like a rock.

VIDEO: HE POINTS TO A RIP IN HIS PANTS

AUDIO: A dog ripped my pants...and you know, I still don't think half of them believe me.

VIDEO: HE MAKES A FACE, GRASPS HIS STOMACH

AUDIO: It's enough to give a patriot

VIDEO: PAUL"S BODY, THROUGH COMPUTER ANIMATION, DISTENDS WIDELY AND UNDULATES

AUDIO: in-di-ges-tion

VIDEO: BOTTLE OF PEPTO-BISMOL ACROSS SCREEN

AUDIO: ANNOUNCER VOICE OVER: Indigestion? Pepto-Bismol

VIDEO: A CURTAIN OF PEPTO-BISMOL FLOWS DOWN THE SCREEN. TITLE: COATS, SOOTHES, RELIEVES

AUDIO: It coats, soothes, relieves.

VIDEO: MRS. REVERE HANDS PEPTO-BISMOL TO PAUL, WHO LOOKS RESIGNED.

AUDIO: PAUL: I guess I'm just not a night person.

A STORYBOARD, RIGHTLY DONE.
◀

SEDUCTIVELY, not just SHE WINKS. Work on it. Get good at it. Craftsmanship counts. Skill is not necessarily an impediment to genius. On the contrary. Skill is the revealer of genius.

Well what about the legends in the business, you retort, who can't draw or spell? What about Jerry Della Femina, who boasts that he only took one advertising course and failed it? What about my own example of the creative director and his androgynous stick figures? You will most often discover that those craftless legends are hardcore MMMs. In any case, the difficult sales they made back in their artist–writer days would have been greatly facilitated by skillful renditions, and some of the sales they didn't make, they might have.

Where were we? Right, you were presenting to the creative director. Consider his imperative—forwarding sellable advertising to clients, yes, but beyond that. The creative director is responsible for the agency reel. The more impressive the reel, the better he's directing the agency's creativity. There is a certain spiritual elevation that invests itself in new creative directors as they seat themselves into the corner chair. Not even the hardest-core MMM who marketed his way to the top is immune. With the smile of the beatified illuminating his countenance, he assembles the department. "New deal around here," he proclaims: "From now on we stand up and fight for our work. Let's start breaking some rules and winning some awards!" His management sponsors who, after all, secured him his chair, now look at him vexed and slightly offended, as Henry must have looked at Becket.

He is your first presentation. You'll want to impress him with three of your abilities: thinking, presenting, creating. You'll achieve the first with your think piece. Write it and read it well, with appropriate timing and eye contact. Three in the bulls-eye, well done. He is now primed for the work, in fact, hoping it's as good as the think piece. You have a magazine ad and a TV storyboard to show him, which you will go about showing in two contrary manners.

A print ad, magazine or newspaper, should speak for itself. If your layout is unmistakable, picture perfect and letter perfect, what is there to explain? Set it before him and wait for the wow.

"Now hold on one moment," you say to me, "about all this perfection. What if I can't draw?" Well then, young friend, you begin with a serious disadvantage. Is that attitude of slinky seduction crucial to your ad? And you've rendered it with a curly circle and one closed eye? Don't count on audience comprehension flooding in and filling the gap. It doesn't happen. What they see is what they get. They'll smile at you weakly as you flounder through your explanation, punctuated by the sound of darts hitting the wall. "You see, the girl is really a sexy siren, not like the drawing, who . . . who. . . ." Thud. If you can't draw, go to art school and learn to draw. Meantime there's some trickery and deceit you might try, such as using reference scrap. Find a photo of a slinky winker in a magazine and clip it to your layout. Even then you never find exactly the right picture, so you'll be explaining the explanation. "See this? It's sort of what our photo will look like, but not quite." Think of the impression you're making on your creative director. Unless he's one who can't draw either.

Right. You presented the print and you won your wow. Now for the television. Same process? No! NEVER, repeat NOT EVER, set a storyboard in front of your audience and say, "Here's the TV." Here's why. While a print layout should be a reasonable simulation of a printed page, a storyboard can't come close to simulating a film. A film is action, music, performance. A storyboard is lines on paper. Conveying the action and music and the performance of your intended film to your audience is a critical test of your presentation skill, which is a critical part of your creative skill. A good film badly conveyed may seem to your audience a lot like a bad film. Hold the board so it's facing you and you're facing the audience, then do the movie! Walk through the action, sing the song, play all the parts. Use some theatrical devices. Conscript your audience to participate. Prerecord your music, or if it's a popular song, buy the cassette. Run through it one more time so you know they're really feeling it, and then and only then show them the board. That way when they see your words and drawings they can easily convert them to film.

Again, good drawings are vital. You don't want to be apologizing that a frame isn't exactly what they'll see. Remember that your board will be making solo appearances without you there to introduce it. Good drawings will ensure that it speaks for itself.

Now let's invite the—what's that you say? You can't draw, you can't sing, and you're petrified in front of people? I see. Let me ask you this —do you have a chauffeur's license? Only kidding, but not completely. There are those in the business who can't either, but the good ones can.

Now let's invite the account folks in.

So it's root root root for the home team, if they don't win it's a shame. It's known as the home-court advantage, and that is the name of the game. There's more to it than the cheers of the paying faithful; it's the personality of the arena. Your tradition lives there, your banners hang there, the seats are painted your colors. You're confident there. All of that is what's lacking to the visitors. They're amid alien traditions, alien banners. They are ever so slightly off-balance.

Therefore take heed: Always present creative work at home. In your office. Your tradition lives there, your books, your Talking Heads poster, your awards. The vibes are right. You're confident. It's not that you seek to discommode the account folks. It's just that you're the one who has to stand up and perform, and you want the home-court advantage.

You can't always have it, of course, with senior account people and clients, but try for the next best thing—the creative director's office or at least a neutral conference room. There will be times when nothing can save you and you'll have to present in his arena amid his books and pictures of his wife. Take a deep breath and be wonderful.

Well, they're seated, go ahead. Present away. Recall now that you're among friends. Haven't you sat in discussion with this bright likable account supervisor and his bright likable exec? Haven't you conspired on the procreation of this idea? It's time now to deliver the advertising. Walk up the thought steps that led to it, read your setup, then lay the magazine ad before them. Wow. Now the television. Same show, dialogue, song, and histrionic devices. (It should improve with each performance.) Wow again.

They like it, a lot. They say so. (This is the second best moment of moments in the business.) But they probably have some suggestions. Listen attentively. Their only motive is to make the work as good as it can be. Which doesn't mean you have to agree with them. If you don't, discuss the point. Resolve it. Leave no issue pending between you. Leave the room firmly allied.

Writer to writer note: If you've written a line that's clever but tricky and it draws stares instead of smiles, reconsider it. Remember, these folks are *trying* to like it. Nobody else from here on will be. It's aggravating to lose one you like, believe me I know, but think of it this way: Remember telling a hilarious joke and nobody at the table got it? And they were good humor people? It wasn't them. It was the joke.

There may be a third internal presentation, to the agency bigshots. There certainly will be if you're developing new thinking or a new strategy. Something else is new. From here on, in this meeting and the client meetings to follow, you'll be presenting as an allied front, you and your account folks. They'll do the preview and the overview, you'll do the setup and the advertising, they'll do the review. This is your first appearance together and it draws applause. Big wows from the big shots. Your next performance will be a road show.

In the client's conference room, the seating is as follows: You and your account folks on one side of the table, the brand supervisor and brand executive and maybe an assistant on the other. Two factors are critical to the success of this presentation. Naturally the quality of the work is, but so too is the quality of your account supervisor. If he's good he's not only anticipated everything anyone may ask, he's set up his co-captain. While you've been working on the advertising, he's been working on the client. By meeting time he has her listing 40 degrees in the right direction.

The show follows the third agency format: preview, overview, setup, advertising, review. Again, watch their faces as he previews and over-views. Do some anticipating of your own. Alter a word or action to suit the situation. You know these players too. Play to them, especially to the power.

Show's over and the client likes it. She has a few questions and the others have a few more. Your account supervisor fields most of them, maybe deflects a few your way. Your fielding is flawless. They all like the work, a lot. They'll take it upstairs.

The fifth and last presentation is the easiest and the hardest. It's easiest because the brand supervisor has joined the allies and because her management won't be finding fault with your words or pictures. They'll be assaying the work against higher ideals such as corporate policy, criteria visible only from lofty elevations, and that's what makes this the hardest meeting. Since nobody down under can foresee the problem, suddenly it's there and it's fatal. Usually there'll be an agency biggie present to deal with the problem if one arises and in truth one seldom does but when it does, it's a crusher. To come all this way and then crunch. Ouch.

Not this time. Big smiles from on high and you're home free. Go produce.

One moment before you do. Of course you realize that for purposes of expediency we've idealized the action. In separate chapters we've assigned you both roles, bright likable account supervisor and talented tenacious creative supervisor, so that you could witness firsthand how the process should function. But pause a moment and replay the same scenes with a Credit Taker as account supervisor or a Midnight Oiler or, saints preserve us, a junior troglodyte. It would have been a different story. You as talented tenacious Artful Detective might, for example, have collided with an MO over a change in strategy, you might have been denied access to the client or your quest for facts, or you might have been mangled in a power play over credit for the idea or victimized by bad fielding at the presentation table. You'd have needed your deepest reserves of reason, resourcefulness, fact, guile, even flattery, and if they didn't work, fiery grit. And you still might not have succeeded. (See point about AD imperative having few perpetrators.)

But, heaven be praised, all of that is what didn't happen. You and your enlightened allies carried the day. Well done. Go ahead now, produce a winner.

9

*P*RODUCTION

*T*here is a third clause to the Artful Detective's imperative. First, determine the brand's most persuasive aspect. Second, create dazzling advertising behind it. Third, strive on to produce a breathtaker on the screen or on the page.

No one, not even you who created it, can entirely envision the final film from the storyboard, nor the final page from the layout. There is magic to be made in the meantime. First you need to hire the magic makers, then you need to seize the magic when it happens, then you need to insist it into the work.

The magic makers. The photographer who takes that one-in-a-million picture that steals your breath. The model with the one-in-a-million wink so contagious you can't help winking back. The film director who lights a scene as a scene hasn't been lit before or who shoots a scene that wasn't in the storyboard, but when you see it in the film, that's the moment when you cease breathing.

And you. Will you know that magic moment when you see it? Sure you will. You'll guide it past objection onto the page or into the film. Objection? What objection, you wonder; who could object to magic? You'd be surprised.

There is a sage and venerable gentleman named Norm Levy who carries a weighty reel of commercials around to Procter & Gamble's agencies every year. He offers numerous examples of rough-produced films that score as well as or better than the same films fully produced. P&G is constantly in the process of considering new campaigns for all its brands, constantly testing new candidate ideas for national advertising. It would break the bank to test all these ideas in fully produced form, so several less-than-fully formats have been developed. These range from photomatics, real sound and music but still photos on film, down to video storyboards—made by literally filming the drawings on the storyboard and adding a soundtrack. Winning candidates are then remade as real films, at real-film prices. Norm will argue, citing one instance after another of the rough version outscoring the slick version, that it's the content that counts and that big-budget film values are lost on the public.

Allow me, friend Norm and friends all, to draw another conclusion from the same evidence: No magic was made in that meantime between the storyboard film and the final film. What they saw in the board film was what they got in the real film, only that and nothing more. Why so?

In some cases there's no room allowed for magic. The idea is too pat, too flat, too predictable. One of those on-strategy but boring ideas we talked about that survives its way through the process to become a boring film that not even Spielberg could alchemize.

However. Even—this is the surprising part—even in cases where magic is allowed for, even when it *strikes,* there on the set, SHAZAM, all too often it meets with indifference! Why? Precisely because it wasn't in the storyboard film. That's not what we agreed on, someone says, and someone else agrees. But it's *better* than what we agreed on, you insist, your eyeballs wide in disbelief. "We don't know that," they say, "let's just go with what we agreed on."

It happens, honest. You do have recourse most of the time. They'll usually let you do it both ways, so you might lose today but win tomorrow. Keep insisting. Utilize that same tact, that same guile, that same grit. You'll win more than you lose.

But wait a second, what are we talking about? Nothing resembling that horrific vision could occur on this project, not with your enlightened account and client allies on the job. They realize all too well that creativity doesn't cease with the storyboard. They, like you, are in the mood for magic.

I've been admiring your virtuosity as we've moved through these pages together. You've been both a man and a woman. You've been an agency partner. You've been an account supervisor and a media and a research person. When we came to creative, you were the Artful Detective on the quest, you were the equally artful presenter and copywriter. That leaves only one part unplayed. Let's have a look at you as art director.

Generally, of the two, art director and writer, it's the writer who's the front person. The one who connects with the account folks, sits in on client strategy sessions, composes the setups, performs the presentations, all the functions you've been handling throughout this chapter. It's generally that way. Two-thirds of the time, I'd say. Where does that leave you as the art director then, generally? Moving in a constant cycle between creation and production. Conceive the idea, prepare the materials, produce the work. Repeat and repeat. The first two you do in concert with your partner. Production is largely your show.

That magazine ad. It's there in your mind, on a page in your mind, the vision of what you intend. It's good, but it could be better. It could be magic. You start by shopping for photographers. Portfolios pour in and you pore over them, looking for that million-to-one touch. Him. Maybe him. Maybe her. You summon the three photographers' reps and ask them to bid on the job. Not only how much will it be, but how will it be done? Which one has the magic touch? The bids are in. One of the three has the best price and the best answer combo, and that's the one who gets the job.

That is, presuming the client signs the estimate. DO NOTHING, expend not a farthing, until the brand manager has approved the estimate. An over-the-phone okay can too easily be rescinded when the bills come in. ("Nine thousand? I thought you said *five* thousand.") Get it in ink.

Now the model. Nearly always it's the photographer who casts for talent, although nothing says you can't too. Have you seen that face in your mind in another ad? In a commercial, in a movie, on the bus? You mull through hundreds of models' composites like a victim scanning mugshots. You find a hundred maybes. You pare them down to twelve, to six. The six come in for test shots, and then it's only one. That one.

There gather now the several people you have portrayed so admirably, for what is called the preproduction meeting. In a long-table conference room with VCR, coffee urn and cookies, client, account, and creative people shake hands and take chairs. It may be the only occasion all year when all of the yous get together, except maybe the Christmas party. You've gathered to discuss all aspects of the production. And who are these other folks? Has everyone met everyone? This is Mark, our photographer; Ellen, our stylist; Marian, our home economist; and Ginny, she does wardrobe.

The first order of business is casting. You'll propose your number-one model choice, expecting the client to agree, but you'll have numbers two and three in your pocket just in case. Then you'll go over every other detail of the ad—the model's hairdo, her blouse, even her wedding ring. The food, how much lettuce. The product, what angle. The background curtains, the clock, whether there's a toaster on the counter. It's astounding what disputes can arise over what seem trivialities, but better they erupt around the table than on the set.

On the set it's you and the photographer. An account person will be there, very likely with the client, and they'll probably stay for the duration, patient souls. Your copywriter may show up, mostly to show his face. These sessions tend to endure for hours, and writers are not famous for their Zenlike concentration. Doesn't matter. You two are all that matters. You and the photographer making magic. You shoot Polaroids first, large-format color pictures that provide a pretty good preview. They're okay with account and client? Go for it. First you shoot the exact layout picture, to cover your lower back. If it lacks magic, widen your sights. Still no? Call time out. Huddle with the photographer. Swap ideas. Sketch. Invent. Come back to the set with a fresh approach. Click, no. Click, no. Click, yes. Magic. You've got it on the roll and you know it.

Next day your chromes are back from the lab, 8×10 and gorgeous. There's your magic, on not one but three exposures. You propose the best of the best to account and client, they agree, you move on to the retouching. No best is ever so best that it's perfect. There's always retouching. (Well, almost always.) The product is a little too orange. The lettuce is a little too wilted. The model's two little bumps are showing. Little things are easily repaired, with chemicals applied like paint right onto the chrome. For drastic repair, a dye transfer is made. That's a positive of the negative enlarged to 16×20. Alterations are performed on the positive, then a new negative is shot from it. The retouched photo is sent to the engraver with the mechanical for positioning and cropping.

With the what? While the retoucher was simulating perfection, you were selecting a typeface and setting type for the copy. With the type, the logo, and a photostat of the photo, you put together a dummy ad that's called a mechanical. Don't ask me where they got mechanical. Same place they got kumquat.

The engraver takes another photo of your photo and translates it to color separation film. That's a mysterious process involving four plates of the four primary colors. He then sends you a first proof and you check it for color and tone. Too blue? Too dense? Too orangey? You send it back for color correction, then you send the revised proof around for approval. This is the last shot everybody gets at the ad before the printer prints.

Above all, make sure you do what you need to to produce your personal best work. Even if it gets re-revised or even refused, you know you did it right. Keep a copy of your version for your portfolio.

Right. Print down, TV to go.

Time now to introduce a new character into our narrative. She, let's say she's a she since she probably is, is someone you as an art director know well but some of our other readers haven't had the pleasure of meeting. She is that remarkably skillful and responsible creative person known as the agency producer. But before she steps forward, a bit of background.

Corollary to the advertising-agency business is the vast industry of film and tape production, centered in Los Angeles and New York. At the epicenter of the industry stands the film production house, with its roster of star directors. Slightly below it in renown is the videotape house, and beneath these extends an array of support facilities: houses of editing, recording, composing, animating, casting, and finishing.

A most valuable member of the production-house staff is the producer, sister to our own agency producer. Her job is, tersely stated, to pull the production together. She begins at the top of the process, helping to prepare the bid. One drawback to being awarded a bid is that you really have to shoot the film for as little as you said you would. That is her first and abiding problem, having so much to do and so little to spend. She calls first her own people then the agency producer and clarifies for all how she plans to proceed.

Item one: Prepare a schedule. Day by day, from first phone call through final wrap.

Item two: Engage a crew. Electricians, set designers, lighting people, props, wardrobe, makeup, styling, production assistants. She hires the best, and if not, then the best she can find, and it's always a matter of chance. He's in Majorca, she's having her cat spayed, he's on a Pampers job.

Item three: Bring it in on time and budget. No, tell the set designer we can't afford that much, he'll have to design a simpler set. The good stage isn't available, we'll have to take a worse one at a higher price. Grab it, the next alternative is worse yet.

Item four: Remain in tight touch with the agency producer. Keep each other informed of progress and availabilities.

Item five: The preproduction meeting. Same table, same coffee urn, same client–agency cast as for the print shoot, with the addition of our agency producer and the film house people.

Our agency producer enters the process a few days after the client approves the job. You and your writer acquaint her with the history of the new thinking and the purpose it means to serve. You include any promises you may have made along the way. You take the action and the angles, the intention of each frame. Your writer partner discusses dialogue, delivery, word emphasis, music. The three of you speculate over directors, acting talent, music houses. Make it clear that what you have on cardboard is good. What you have in mind is magic.

You'll seek your wizardry in that cluster of enchanted castles called film production houses. The wizards resident there, the commercial film directors, are a variegated lot, ranking from genuine dazzle-doers to seedy slicksters, frayed at the sleeve. But don't moisten your eye for them—the least among them earns $4000 a day for his work, the best around $7500. Yes, a day. What's that you say? You're switching your major? Not yet. Know first that a goodly number of film directors apprenticed as art directors.

So your producer calls in the reels. You sit together viewing wizardry commissioned by other people for other projects and you try to apply it to your own. That lighting, that angle, that action. You sit through 20 reels, then 20 more, pausing, reversing to see that scene again, then you've got it. Three circles around three names. You call in your writer and your supervisor for endorsement. They agree. Your producer will call in those directors' reps for bids.

At this point your supervisor may or may not ask the account and client folks in for corroboration. He ought to, and if he's the man we know him to be, he will. There are those who won't, who'll stall and dodge through the entire production process, their backs against a flimsy door holding account and client out. It's that same attitude of "leave us alone to do our work," and it is, as always, hopelessly deluded. You *want* the client and the account people with you. You want their approbation, move by move. It eliminates a negative: If they have an objection, it's made now, not in the screening room. And it accentuates a positive: They are on your side if someone else, even their management, raises an objection.

Don't worry that their presence will inhibit your genius. Feel free to flourish it. Be brilliant. They'll admire you all the more.

Back to the movie. While the bids are out, the talent comes in. The producer has conferred with the casting people, whether in-house or independent, explaining what you have in mind. The call goes out and in they come. Several people, sometimes dozens, on occasion hundreds, will be summoned to try out for one role. Passing through the lobby of an agency's casting floor, it's not uncommon to find 30 nearly identical performers there seeking the same part. Thirty 30-year-old blow-dried blondes rehearsing the same line to themselves: "This new Charmin is even softer!" With appropriate gestures. A unique vision.

With the producer and casting person, you'll cull down the dozens of aspirants to 10 possibles. You and your partner will narrow the number to three, call in the supervisor for approval, then call the three back for one more look.

But look—the three film house bids are in. As with the print, one of the three bids will offer the best price combined with the best point of view. Which one? That one. You've selected your director.

Now call the three talent selections back and show the director the call-back tapes. He deserves a vote, and he may have worked with one or two of them before. You consult, you decide. Now two elements are in place with one to go: the music.

Advertising music. You've been hearing it for years, on local radio and big-time television. I'll bet you can sing 11 jingles from memory. Go ahead, sing one. Sometimes they're admirably thoughtful, like "Reach out and touch someone," but, "I'm a Pepper, you're a pepper"? "Coke is it"? Who couldn't have written "Coke is it"? Who does write this stuff?

The answer is, lots of people. It's another vast industry corollary to advertising, ranging from little guys with guitars to colossal factory studios with more control panels than NASA and more black boxes than the Grateful Dead.

You listen to a passel of sample cassettes and bid three music houses, the three who make the sort of sounds you and your partner have been hearing in your heads. Each house submits a demo tape, a few instruments carrying the melody and tempo. You listen, listen again, and choose. With the director, the talent, and the music house signed on, you're one step from rolling camera. That step? The preproduction meeting. Come in, everyone, and welcome. Account supervisor you sit here, brand supervisor there, execs here and there, creative supervisor, writer, art director. Meet our director, our assistant director, and our studio producer. This is Ginny, she'll be doing the wardrobe, and Doug, he's our set designer.

That was the agency producer doing the intros, and she'll go on chairing the meeting as every item is examined in detail. The action, the words, the camera angles, the set, the talent, the clothes, the music, any special effects or finishing touches, all of it is discussed to everyone's satisfaction. A schedule is passed out, hands are shaken all around, nice to meet you, see you on the set.

At this point we say good-bye to our studio producer. She hands her job folder over to the on-set foreman, the assistant director, and moves along to her next production. Sorry to see her go, but that's the job cycle of the film company producer.

If you wouldn't mind, I'd like to promote you again, pro tem, to make a point. May I? Thank you. You're creative supervisor again.

The moment client management gave approval to produce, the mantle of responsibility passed to your shoulders. You are now the one who best sees all the pieces of the project. You were there at the inception of the idea, the conception of the executions, and presentations up the line. You are the only one cognizant of all these component factors, as well as client desires, fears, and politics, as well as the intricacies of the production process. Stay on top of it all. There'll be personality clashes, bruised vanities, off-the-wall suggestions, cost overruns during the shooting, and all of them could be hazardous to the health of the film. Deal with them. Resolve them. Use your famous charm or reason or fiery grit, as needed. *Work it out.* Your allies are counting on you. Remember that in the screening room, when the lights come back on, all looks will be directed your way. Whether they'll be smiling or scowling looks depends on how you handle the unpredictabilities of this production. Excuses fall flatter than bad soufflés. Deliver what you sold them, plus magic. That and nothing less.

Capito? Good. Hold still, I'll pin the old insignia back on. While you're holding let me clear up these function vagaries of art director, writer, and creative supervisor. The supervisor is of course either a writer or an art director, either active or elevated. If he's active, then he's one of the partners. He's the copywriter *and* the supervisor, working with an art director, or he's the art director *and* the supervisor, working with a writer. Usually the former, as we've mentioned. If he's elevated, then he only supervises. Does he research, does he present? Perhaps. That depends on how high he chooses to elevate. Knowing you, you'd probably be a hands-on supervisor, in touch all the way. Okay? They're waiting for you on the set.

There's a code of protocol on the set that reads like one of Moses's tablets. Neither art director nor writer nor supervisor may address the director directly. All observances must be relayed through the agency producer. What if the talent is reading the line incorrectly? Writer whispers to producer who whispers to director who instructs talent. Naturally, like rumors, observances change shape with each transfer so the director's instructions may only partially resemble the writer's wishes. Does this strike you as one of those elements potentially hazardous to health of the film? It is. There is a better way to go around it—I mean about it.

Long before you step onto the set with the director, make an effort to get next to him personally. Go have a wine with him, have dinner with him, you and the writer and the producer. You liked his work, you'll probably like him, and he'll probably want to meet the pair who authored this marvelous board. Remember that he only walked into this job yesterday, and he'll walk away from it day after tomorrow. Who among us could absorb all the hopes and intentions and fears and inflections that live inside a storyboard, just by reading over the photostat? No one whose pronoun isn't capitalized. Your director should be pleased to hear you out in detail, pleased to establish cordial relations with you. It can only mean an even better film, harmony on the set, and that you'll think of him highly the next time around.

Now it's film morning and you meet on the set as new friends instead of nodding acquaintances. If the director has questions during the filming, he'll call you over and ask, you or the producer or the writer. If you have suggestions, wait for a break and call him over. Should you hit an impasse, ask him to take five while the four of you discuss it.

Impasses on this set? With this board and all this talent, all new friends? Scarce. When the director calls the final *Cut!* and pronounces the film a wrap, you'll lounge about with a glass of Soave and regale one another for a mission well accomplished and vow you'll bid him on the next one.

Next day you view the results. Ten, 15 takes of exactly the same scene, but not exactly. Tiny differences of motion, emphasis. You select the takes you prefer in concert with the writer, the producer, and your next new friend, the film editor. This is the moment you know whether or not you have canned some magic. Yes, that's the one. Take six. You knew you had it and there it is. That take is going to win you a Clio.

Next scene, the editing studio. You three and your editor skillfully piece the takes together to form the film, working the cuts against the music. There are two ways to marry music to picture. The ideal way is a trial marriage, cutting the film to that demo music track, then recording the full track to the finished picture. The usual way is the less expensive way, recording the full track first then cutting the picture to it, in the mode of a music video.

Finishing touches are recording the announcer voiceover, color correcting as with the print, and finishing. The finishing is done at a tape transfer studio where those graphics like supers and titles you see in commercials ("Use only as directed") are added.

Then the lights go out. The film presentations replicate the storyboard presentations, creative director through client management. As before, your account supervisor and brand supervisor stand with you as allies because they've stood with you as participants through the entire production process.

They love it. They all love it. They stand and ovate. You made magic.

10

GETTING TO
BE ONE

*W*ell, which one will it be? Producer? Art director? Copywriter?

Of the three, in fact of all of the jobs in advertising, the job of film
producer is the one job you can't obtain directly. That is, you can't
come in, apply for the job, be accepted, and start Monday. Getting to
be one can be a haphazard, frustrating process, which is why I didn't
assign you the role. But, if you insist, here goes. Most agencies these
days have a sort of apprentice program, starting you as a production

secretary or an assistant in casting or cost control. After a year or so, when you're familiar with the system, especially the cost-control system, you're moved up to assistant producer. Be aware that there is ferocious competition for these jobs. You need to come equipped with learning, proper personality, perseverance, and good fortune.

Learning. Take college courses in film and video, with emphasis on the production, not the performance, end. Not that starring in the class movie would impair your progress, but don't be deluded. The job of producer, agency or studio, is a lot more arithmetic than it is show business. Anything and everything you can do in a behind-the-camera capacity—budgeting, lighting, propping, casting, editing, sound mixing —it all counts. That goes for class projects and especially for outside projects. It always looks impressive on a résumé that you've accomplished something beyond the curriculum. There are always shoestring films being shot. Help produce one, even for no wages. Work a summer at a TV station or a radio station.

When you're ready to come looking, open that red book and write to the heads of production at a bunch of agencies, but don't stop there. Scour the trade press for go-fer jobs at studios. Chase down every chance. It really doesn't matter if you start at a studio or an agency. As we've seen, the studio producer's and the agency producer's jobs are very similar. Interchange is frequent. Most producers I know have worked both camps. The important thing is to get started somewhere.

Impress your interviewer with your ability to organize—most of the producer's job consists of putting things together. And with your patience and flexibility. Conditions change back and forth and back again on less than a moment's notice. Stalwart principles and flaring egos are liabilities in the film business.

Be persistent, be resourceful. Remember that there are a hundred wide-eyed aspirants for every open post. Film production is, after all, a glamorous profession. Veteran producers will scoff at the term, but it is more glamorous than most jobs—making wrenches, for example. Good luck. You'll need it.

Or would you prefer art directing? Or copywriting?

First, a tale of two boroughs. Some several years ago I was engaged by a famous art school to teach an advertising course. The institute's reputation was enhanced by the renown of its graduates in fine arts, engineering, and architecture. Set beside these lofty endeavors, advertising seemed indeed a trivial pursuit. Certainly it did to the institute deans. Their artists drawing roach traps? Pickle jars? Panty hose? Worse than demeaning. (Only Andy Warhol could mix fine art with soup.) Yet some of their students were calling for advertising courses, assuming that the pay would be better in agencies than in ateliers. In fact the school had offered art direction courses in the past, taught by idle architects out of thick texts. They'd been, as we've mentioned, worse than useless. But what was the remedy?

The school was in Brooklyn, slightly too far from Madison Avenue to lure pros over after work. Well, if the teachers couldn't come to the college, maybe the students could come to the agency. That was our arrangement. Every Tuesday evening from 6 to 8, twenty art students arrived for Mr. Caffrey's class on Advertising Concepts. What the business is about. Who does what and how they do it together. How to conceive, execute, and present an ad. Something like this book.

Their term projects would be their personal portfolios. Everyone seeking an art director or copywriter position at an agency must present a portfolio—a dozen or so sample ads in a looseleaf binder known simply as *the book*. What more perfect term project could there be than the essential credential for getting a job?

All semester we labored. Each week I'd present the facts in a different product case. We debated and discussed until we felt we were totally familiar with every aspect of the product. Twenty artful detectives in the making. The next week they'd present their ads. Their work was judged on quality of thinking, execution, and presentation. It was usually long past 9 before they'd turn me loose, and I understood why. They were hungry to know more and more about the business they might be entering, and this was their one contact with a living practitioner earning a living in the subject he was teaching.

At the end of the term, each student possessed a good portfolio, rightly done. Naturally, some were superior to others, but almost all were good enough to get jobs behind. It was school policy for all graduating students to present their term projects in their major subjects to the faculty review committee. Mine did and I was fired. Their portfolios, I was informed by a dean, were not art-school term projects. They were business-school projects. My students' projects were unworthy of the school. I was unworthy of the school. My students protested (it was the era) to no avail. I was not asked back.

And what might be the point of this humiliating history? Just this. Given (1) the tepid esteem accorded advertising by the academic fraternity and (2) the general unavailability of front-line teachers, you, student, are in serious peril of approaching your chosen profession as an educated unemployable.

Hear this and hear it clearly. Unless you have a good portfolio rightly done, you will not get a job in advertising as an art director or as a copywriter. Marks, honors, papers, elective office, they count zero without the book. So let's get to it.

Who will look at your book? First, a placement agent. There is a satellite business to our business known as headhunting. Attractive ladies of a post-meridiem age they are, nearly all, and if one of them esteems your book well enough to send it on rounds, you'll have saved ten thousand steps. Second, an agency creative personnel person, in age and outlook, sister to the placement agent, employed by the agency personnel department, assigned to the creative department. She will have alerted the agent that an art director or writer is wanted at a certain level at a certain salary. She will seldom render judgment on your book unless it is egregiously fine or foolish. Third, a creative director. He or she will have alerted the agency personneler that an art director or writer is wanted in his or her group. He or she will do the judging and the hiring.

Does every placement agency treat with beginners? No.

What if no agent will accept your book? Than you and your Hushpuppies will take it on rounds.

Does every agency have a creative personnel person? No, smaller agencies usually do not. Sometimes even in agencies that do, creative directors deal directly with placement agents.

What will a creative director be looking for, looking at your book? A new employee who can bring new thinking to the permanent product problems of his group. Keep in mind that you are young. Fresh. Unscarred. A creative director will not be looking for solid safe ideas, competently executed. He has shelves of competency in his group. Bales of it. He's looking for zest. He's looking for fire. Fire can always be brought under control. Igniting competency, that's a problem.

How many ads should you feature? About 12 different products. Doubles or triples on one or two if you like, so about 15 insertions in all.

Should you feature campaigns of three ads, to demonstrate your campaign thinking? Do it once, maybe twice, no more. The product concept and the executional idea require hardcore thinking. Look-alike ads are softcore. Four campaigns of three ads each do not constitute a portfolio.

All print, no radio or TV? Mostly print. Magazine ads or newspaper ads read instantly. If you have a crusher of a radio or TV idea that will not be denied inclusion in the book, include it. But make it easy to understand. Good drawings. Video directions. (You'll find a sample storyboard on page 86.)

You're a writer and you can't draw, so what do you do? Find someone to help you lay out the ads and draw the visuals. I don't know how, barter something. Cook a dinner, write a paper, loan your car, pay if you have to, but get it done. Do *not* exhibit a blank page with "Blue flower goes here." Reach out and find someone to draw you a flower.

You're an art director and you can't write? Two choices. Get some help, even a whole-book collaborator. Or do the best you can. If your visual concepts are stunning, if your layout and design are impressive, a creative director will overlook your imperfect prose.

Is choosing the right products important? It's critical. Your choices will determine whether your portfolio rises and shines or flops. Whether it hits on the first try or goes about making continual agency rounds unclaimed like the last forgotten suitcase on an airport carousel.

What sort of products should you choose? Do not choose high-visibility high-budget items like Coke and Ford and Tide. Thousands of creative groups over the years have worn their pencils short on cars and colas and detergents, issuing forth millions of ideas, both fine and foolish. Any idea you have will probably have been had before, maybe by the reader. Don't compete. (Unless your idea is bona fide brilliant, then by all means have at it.) Do not choose no-budget items either, like forest fires or crippled children. Anybody can create a heartbreaking ad for a worthy cause. It's just too easy. Choose products with smaller budgets, products with unsatisfactory advertising, products that need a new look. In the next section we'll set forth case histories on 10 products for a rise-and-shine portfolio.

Do they need to be real products? Yes, all real. Unless your invention is cause for applause in itself. And all legal and practical restraints apply as well. Don't claim the product can do what it can't. Don't ashcan the competition. Don't call for celebrities you can't afford or who wouldn't do it. Stay within a budget reasonable for the product.

A diversion on legality: I'm sure that cynical mind of yours assumes that advertisers today all claim their products can do what they can't, left and right. They don't. Not that some of them wouldn't like to, but they aren't allowed to. The Federal Trade Commission has a lot of laws against it. Which came about because advertisers years ago did just that. Here's an array of grievous offenders from Lyman's day (see opposite page).

Naturally there were honest merchants then who advertised their products accurately, and to them we tip our hat because their only restraint was character. Legally they were perfectly free to misinform and misrepresent like their larcenous colleagues. There were no laws, no government forces to protect people from these arrogant frauds. Nor did the media refuse their wares, supposing, I suppose, that fools who believed something would restore eyesight or cure epilepsy or grow hair deserved to be parted from their money so why lose a sale, and who knows, it's the age of miracles, maybe some of the stuff really works.

These days good character has some potent legal aid, but it's taken decades to exorcise the charlatans. In the forties Lucky Strike cigarettes were making a health claim! "Not a cough in a carload," they announced. In the sixties Geritol claimed it remedied "tired blood." What was tired blood? That's what the FTC wanted to know, by then fully in

TRUTH IN ADVERTISING IN 1902.

place and asserting its power. Of course Geritol would take any interpretation a viewer inferred, preferably a diminution of youthful vigor in middle age, preferably sexual. But since Geritol wouldn't do diddly for those departed powers, how could they defend their advertising? They stalled and litigated for 14 years before agreeing to a fine of $280,000.

By the mid-seventies the FTC had grown full height, and when they read that Listerine killed germs that cause colds, they hit the siren. That advertising, they ruled, implies that Listerine lessens or curtails colds. Does it? Not that Listerine could prove. The brand was ordered to issue "corrective advertising" stating that Listerine could not reduce the incidence or severity of colds, and to spend $10.6 million doing it, the same amount they'd spent claiming it could.

These days, if you make a claim about your product you'd better be prepared to prove it, and that's good. It means that everybody plays by the same rules. It means that people get to judge products on their merits, not on some *gonif*'s evil imagination.

An amusing incident to conclude.

Years ago at Young and Rubicam, I wrote TV and radio commercials for Piels Beer. They featured two cartoon brothers, Bert and Harry Piel, voiced by the comedy team Bob and Ray, who were the imaginary owners of the brewery. It was a fun but full-time job, requiring a dozen television and about 50 radio spots a year. Many of them used real people's names. See, Bert was a personable little entrepreneur and he ran his business in a personal way. He'd never hesitate to harangue a friend over the air for using a competitor's product, for example. "David Bain!" he might say. "How many years do we go back, David? Didn't I get you your *Saturday Evening Post* route? And what do I hear? You were seen at Fred Wyshak's barbecue with a can of Brand X? Don't tell me you were just keeping it warm!" Legally, I needed a $1 signed release form from a real David Bain and from a real Fred Wyshak. It was easy. Everybody in the agency and company and all of my friends were delighted to hear their names in a Bert and Harry commercial. All I needed was a signed release and I was licit. Or so I thought.

One day I was concocting a radio script about the good old days. The brothers were reminiscing. "Harry," Bert says, "remember that

How do you *fight a Cold?*

Nose drops often help relieve congestion ...
anti-histamines, aspirin, cough syrups can help.
But remember ... these non-antiseptic
cold remedies don't kill germs the way
Listerine Antiseptic does ... and germs cause
much of the misery of colds and the sore throats
they bring. Listerine kills germs instantly ...
by millions. No matter what else you do
for a cold—use Listerine Antiseptic!
Use it full-strength!

At the first sign of a cold ...

Listerine Antiseptic—Quick!

LISTERINE: $10.6 MILLION CLAIMING IT COULD,
THEN $10.6 MILLION MORE ADMITTING IT
COULDN'T.

society guy with the Hupmobile? What was his name?" I needed a society name. Something Van Something. I sifted through the roster of Y&R copywriters. Schuyler Van Hooten! Perfect. Schuyler became Bert's society guy. A month later the commercial aired on the radio, and the day after, my creative director received a phone call.

"Charlie Feldman?"

"Speaking."

"This is Schuyler Van Hooten. Senior. I just heard my name in a beer commercial and I don't like it! Where do you come off using my name without my permission? I'm instructing my attorney to bring suit against Piels, against your agency, against you and anybody else I can think of!"

"But we have your son's permission and it's his name too."

"It was mine first and I'm more important!"

He was right about the more important. It is illegal to use a famous person's name, even if you have a release from an unfamous person of the same name, unless you make it clear you're talking about the unfamous one. You couldn't say, for example, that Gerry Ford wears Supphose and Jimmy Carter eats Froot Loops and leave it at that, even if you could produce a bona-fide Ford and Carter. Schuyler Senior was a former heavy-hitter in the stock market, so he had a case. What to do? Charlie called in Schuyler Junior and explained.

"Maybe you don't know this, Charlie," Schuyler told him, "but my dad and I don't get along too well. We haven't spoken for months. Let me try something."

He dialed his father.

"Dad? Schuyler. Listen dad, maybe it's not such a good idea for you to sue Piels . . . . Well, if you sue Piels, then Piels will fire Y&R and Y&R will fire me, and I'll have to come home and live with you. (LONG SILENCE.) Right. You're making the right decision. Bye, dad."

Schuyler Junior smiled. Schuyler Senior had dropped the suit.

And now back to your book.

Should you do just ads, no think pieces, those setup paragraphs so useful in presenting work? Rarely are think pieces found in beginner books, which doesn't mean they aren't a good idea. They are, done rightly. Think your think piece well, keep it short, and set it opposite the ad. It will exhibit your conceptual ability alongside your executional ability. And it will set up the ad for the reader, as you would do if you were there presenting it.

Beyond all other considerations, realize that your book is your advertisement for yourself. It will be read by a highly select group, several people in a position to pay your salary. How do you wish to appear to them? Bold? Smart? Adventurous? Canny? Young? Swift? Deft? Of course. Make it happen just that way. Ad after ad. Cause the reader to put down the book and pick up the phone. "Rosemary? This is the kid we need."

11

TEN CASES
INSIDE ONE

*T*he outside case looks like this:

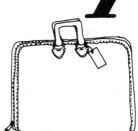

or this:

Soft-cover zip-around looseleaf or hardcover snaplatch. The hardcover case is really just an empty box that pro art directors fill with their mounted and plasticized published ads. Sometimes a buoyant beginner will laminate his layouts and use the hardcover, but not most times. Most times new writers and art directors both favor the soft looseleaf book, with plastic envelopes for pages.

You *might* (understand a discouraging tone in my pencil here) choose to trick up the cover of your book with smile decals or racing stripes to set it apart from the other 500 books making the rounds. You might even letter on it in yellow *Lenny Bagstrap, the new kid in town.* I've seen a few books that weren't books at all but shopping bags or tool boxes. My advice? Resist the temptation. As the homely newlywed said, it's what's between the covers that counts.

And what will you insert between your covers? Here are 10 suggestions.

BUFFERIN

• *BUFFERIN.*   Twenty years ago, before the coming of nonaspirin pain relievers, your store shelf options were five: Bayer Aspirin, Bufferin, Excedrin, Alka-Seltzer, and all others. Aspirin, the wonder drug, is an acid. It can cause hyperacidity in sensitive stomachs. Or, taken in large doses, as for arthritis, in any stomachs. So Bufferin, buffered aspirin, was developed. The formula blends aspirin with alkaline to minimize hyperacidity and, theoretically at least, to dispatch more aspirin faster into the bloodstream and on to the pain. Watch a Bufferin commercial on the advertising Hall of Fame reel, and you'll see little animated B letters beating A letters to the pain every time. Well, if a pain reliever with buffered aspirin is better than plain aspirin, then a pain reliever with no aspirin has to be best of all, right? Enter Tylenol and its several siblings. But wait a minute, is that premise correct? When you omit aspirin, you're omitting one of the truly remarkable pain relievers of modern times. Nothing matches it for reduction of inflammation, therefore fever and even headache. Those thousand doctors on the desert island made the right choice. But it still upsets stomachs. So why then isn't Bufferin still a valid option? Why not the option of choice?

Do some research at the library. Read about aspirin in the *Readers' Guide to Periodical Literature.* Do some more at the drug store. Read the labels. Compare prices. Form your thoughts into advertising and a think piece. Print or TV.

• *REEBOK.* Ask yourself two questions. Would you like to be running around in Reeboks? Why?

Why, indeed? Reebok is the current rage label, and as with any vanity plate, you pay a premium. (Best vanity plate candidate: on a white VW Rabbit, I'M LATE.) In Reebok's case, is the plate worth the premium? Run over to the shoe merchant in the mall. Do some comparison shopping. Try on Reeboks. Try on Pumas. Adidas. Talk to the salesperson. Ask why Reeboks cost so much more, sometimes twice as much. You may see a Reebok poster in the store explaining the brand's aerobic advantages, and you may find it convincing. One way or another you'll need to justify that premium price in your advertising. If you can't make a thoroughly convincing case for functional superiority, you'll need to augment it with vanity gratification. Consider how other high-dollar tickets have done it. BMW. Rolex. Print only.

STEINWAY & SONS

• *STEINWAY,*   speaking of big tickets. Now you might think that the Steinway name would speak for itself. Don't 95% of all concert pianists choose Steinways? Yes they do, even though many would be given free Yamahas or Baldwins for defecting.

A Steinway grand is in some ways the most remarkable of musical instruments. It contains many thousands of individual pieces and parts, yet it is almost totally constructed, finished, and regulated by hand. Many of its critical parts are Steinway designed and patented, and are found in no other piano. Result: Its tone and touch, its clear powerful voice, simply have no equals.

So sayeth the maker, and professional players are generally in concert. Certainly the headliners are. Horowitz and Serkin expect to see the word above the keys when they sit and flip the tails. Almost all headliners do, most almost-headliners do, and here's where the problem begins to set in. As the headlines diminish, the willingness to pay the Steinway price does too. There are only so many Serkins around. Steinway must sell pianos down deeper into the playing public. But have you seen the sale price? $6000 for a Steinway upright. $3000 for a Yamaha. $22,000 for a Steinway living-room grand. $12,000 for a Yamaha. Is the Steinway difference worth $10,000? Even for those who could pay it without pain, is it worth it?

Your job: Make it worth it. It will be difficult for you to research the subject if you don't live near a Steinway dealer and/or if you don't play, but there isn't much more you need to know. For brochures write to Steinway, 109 West 57 Street, New York, New York 10019. Print or radio.

• *FREIXENET.*

A case of enigmatic champagne. Is it French? Is it Italian? Is it Spanish? Is it imported? How good is it? How good can an imported champagne be if it costs less than California champagne? We have just slipped across that foggy frontier into the mystic land of perception. Champagne, perfume, fashion, cosmetics, even beer reside there. Names on the mailboxes read Gucci, Chanel, Perrier, Dom Perignon. Perception. Read those names over again. They ooze superiority. But are they truly superior? The products without the labels? The same world that pays premium prices for premium-label products often cannot recognize those products when the labels are removed. Test panel after test panel, sniffing perfume sachets, cannot discriminate $100 perfume from $10 perfume. Beer blind-testers fail to judge the famous national brands from cheap local brands. And yet every one of us, you and I included, will insist our senses are acute enough to know the difference between prestige and cheap. If I fill your glass from a bottle of $50 champagne, you'll swear there's nothing as exquisite on earth, even though it's really Freixenet with a paste-on label.

Well if that's the case, what is the superior difference we'd like the world to perceive about Freixenet? What is the world's current impression of Freixenet? How do we move the world from here to there?

Which returns us to our original enigma. We don't *know* what the world currently thinks of Freixenet. French? Italian? Spanish? Imported? Quality? Cheap? You don't know, I don't know, I doubt Freixenet really knows. And how are we going to move the world from here to there if we don't know where here is? Any agency would insist on a research study to determine folks' current impressions of the product. Well, what they can do big, you can do small and have some fun doing it.

Throw a party. A champagne-testing party. Invite five or six couples and ask each to bring a bottle of their favorite champagne. You spring for a costly brand as a taste paragon. Mumm's or Veuve Clicquot or even Dom P. And of course Freixenet. Begin with a questionnaire. Ask your guests to name as many brands of champagne as come to mind, identifying each as domestic or imported. Next, exhibit all the bottles. Take votes on place of origin and price. Next, cover the labels and hold a taste test. Offer each tester three glasses, each glass numbered. Ask the tester to identify the brands.

Next morning when your head clears you'll have all the answers you need. You'll have, in effect, a small-scale version of what the agency researchers would have on their own morning after. You'll have the world's current impression of Freixenet.

Now determine that superior difference you'd *like* the world to perceive about Freixenet. Is it exquisitely fine imported champagne at an affordable price? Maybe you didn't mention price at all. Maybe you refer to your taste test.

And now that you know the here and the there of it, move the world. Print only.

• *YOUR LOCAL BASEBALL TEAM.* In 1986, for the first time in history, every major league baseball team exceeded one million in home attendance. Winners, placers, showers, and also-rans all passed a million souls through their stiles, some well over two million. It was, as Frank says, a very good year. But time out a moment. Let's count up those numbers again. Average attendance, 1.5 million. Average stadium capacity, 55,000. Home games, 81. Potential attendance, 4.45 million. In this all-time record year, the nation's stadiums were, on average, two-thirds empty.

Well, what are you going to do about that? What would you propose if your local baseball team were your client? Major league or minor league, it doesn't matter. Not even the sport matters. Make it football or basketball or hockey if you prefer. What matters is your proposal for filling empty seats.

First consider the team. How good are they, truly? Don't promise a pennant if they can't deliver one. Nothing looks sillier than a last-place team whose stadium banners proclaim *This Is the Year!* Consider the fans. Ask around. Why aren't they taking themselves out to the ball game? Is it something advertising can alter?

If your proposal includes promotion, okay, a good portion of a team's budget is allocated for promotion, cap days and bat days and such, but beware. Make it a practical idea, something the club might really do. Don't call for a contest whose winner pitches the first game, or free tickets to everyone named Homer. And remember it's the ad that counts, not the stunt. Print, maybe radio.

- *RIT DYE.*   It's an idea so old, it sounds new. Used to be, when a woman was bored with her old white curtains, she got herself new blue curtains for the price of the box of Rit. These days she'll just go out and buy new curtains, but why? Same with a blouse or a sweater. Same with a T-shirt or a tablecloth, even sneakers. Dyeing things is a lot easier and cheaper than replacing them. Sounds like a good idea, on paper. Make it look like a good idea in a layout. By the way, resist *Dyeing for a change.* They're using it. Print only.

ARUBA

- *ARUBA.*   For 50 weeks you toil and strain, then hope to God it doesn't rain. Has it happened to you? You work a whole year, save up your getaway dollars, send for a hundred brochures, then pick the wrong place. The weather's rotten or the food is or the people are, but how could you know? It looked so good in the pamphlet.

  Remember those moments when you sat with your folders, trying to decide where to go. Remember them when you sit with your pad trying to decide what to say. What is it about Aruba that makes it an ideal vacation? Your encyclopedia will help, as will your travel agent. Do something that piques the imagination. Something more than sun and sand. Gambling? Weather? Buried treasure? Keep digging, you'll find it. Print or TV.

MONOPOLY®

• *MONOPOLY.* Everyone has a Monopoly game. Don't they? Somewhere around the house? On a closet shelf under the Chinese checkers and the 500-piece jigsaw puzzle of "The Old Mill at Eve"? Or do they? Come to think of it, maybe it's everyone's *mother* who has the Monopoly game. Everyone these days is too busy for Monopoly. After all, it takes two hours to play, and just think what you're missing on TV. Trivial Pursuit maybe, because you can sort of watch with one eye while you're playing, but Monopoly? Too absorbing. And yet, think back. Remember what fun it used to be? Sitting with a hotel on Marvin Gardens and here come the shoe and the hat around Free Parking, heading right at you.

How do you sell a two-hour table game to the channel-switching generation? With some astutely good advertising, of course. Have a go at it. Print and, oh very well, TV.

WHISTLER®

RADAR DETECTORS

- *WHISTLER RADAR DETECTORS.*   This is one product for which the value indisputably justifies the price. I mean, picture it. You're cruising home at 75, confident in your Brand X radar detector, wailing along with Lionel Richie on the FM. Beyond the next hill, a trooper scans his screen. If your fuzz buster doesn't function in time, then the fuzz does the busting and you're $100 lighter with points on your license, and if, by chance, you're cruising home from carousing, you may shortly be walking. That $100 is the difference between a Brand X and a Whistler.

Whistlers locate the law beyond hills, dales, and curves, many crucial seconds before you appear onscreen. They can tell the difference between police cars and ovens. There's even a remote model you can hide under your hood. No wonder half of all truckers with busters own Whistlers.

Convinced? Be convincing. Print only.

- *THE STORE OF YOUR CHOICE.*   This will likely be the most fun but the most work of all. Select a business near you. A store, a restaurant, a lumber yard, a taxi service, a bowling alley. How can you, with advertising, improve the profits of the enterprise? Artful detective, report for duty. You'll need a cooperative owner, of course, but you can offer free advertising in return. Huddle with her or him. Learn all you can learn about the field in general and this business in particular. Does the owner have any notions you might use? Check out the competition. What are they doing better? Talk to customers. Recall how we created advertising for Rowan and for Friar's. Is there a discernible difference to this business? Exploit it. If there isn't, use your inventiveness and create a preference.

If the owner likes your ad, he or she might run it in the local paper. That will give you at least one published page for your portfolio. At the very least, you should come away with a free steak dinner or a free bowling frame or a free two-by-four. Print, of course.

A note on imitation and its penalties. Back in the sixties, the years of sit-ins, draft-card burning, acid and hash, students seemed to major in anger. That first Tuesday night, I waited for their arrival in our agency screening room. Twenty art students coming for classes. Would they occupy the executive floor and issue nonnegotiable demands? Impeach David Ogilvy. Execute Mr. Whipple. In they filed and I looked them over. Long hair, beards, sandals, hairy legs, no bras. When I gave out the assignment I thought, well it won't look much like advertising but it should be refreshing. Surprise. It looked just like advertising, every ad they'd been watching since *Romper Room* with the same old phrases. The key to good value. Great taste. See your local dealer. Do it today.

So much for packaging.

I'd like to assure you that veterans in the business are beyond imitation, but I can't. They aren't. This is a *most* imitative business. The same techniques, the same actors, the same words, over and over again. Even the same character names! Harry. Is there anyone named Harry left in the country? Only in commercials, over and over.

Why? No mystery. Everyone's looking for breakthrough ideas but no one wants to be first. So as soon as someone does break through, everyone else follows rapidly and continuously through the breach.

Understand this now, young reader, as my most earnest plea: Please do not imitate the imitators. Your book should promise fresh fire, not reheated embers. Recheck it for tired words and phrases. Such as?

In our group we have a penal code. Offenders are incarcerated in our agency dungeon, hacked out of the natural rock deep beneath Third Avenue. Offenses and punishment are as follows:

Misdemeanors, 30 days:
Fantastic
Fabulous
Unbelievable
Incredible
Small wonder

Minor felonies, 1 to 5 years:
Kickoff to fall values
Your key to greater savings
Fun in the sun
Delicious and nutritious
Designed with you in mind
It's what [whatever] is all about.
You've tried the rest, now try the best.
[whatever] is our middle name.

Major felony, 15 years to life:
Great taste

After you've rechecked your copy for freshness and accuracy, check it for comprehension. Ask someone, even two someones, if they take out what you put in. Do your words and images mean what you meant? Or don't they? Or worse, do they mean something you didn't mean?

We had a copy supervisor once, a lady grown long of tooth and tight of girdle, who had shunned the depravity of males all her life and remained untainted as Ivory Snow. She was on the Jell-O account, and her assignment was to promote the versatility of the product. After all, Jell-O can be enjoyed any time of day, not just after dinner. She presented an ad featuring a smiling woman saying:

"I gave it to my husband last night and he liked it so much he wanted it again this morning."

And there were none so bold that would tell her no.

Sometimes perfectly clear words aren't. As in the case of the community events editor of our county paper, who composed this headline:

Girl, 17, Takes First Prize in Kennel Show.

12

ORDINARY NASAL SPRAYS: THE WHYS OF BAD ADVERTISING

*W*ell now, you reason, if this book is even reasonably accurate (which it is, reasonably accurate), there seems to be a reasonably reliable methodology for producing excellent advertising. That being the case, you wonder why there's still so much dreck on the air. Why do Marge and Ethyl continue to compare shirts in the laundry room? Why are there diagrams of nostril innards on the screen when you're having dinner? Why is there

Crazy Eddie? And where do they find those primitives who sell storm windows and Toyotas on the off channels?

Wonder no longer. This dreck gets on the air for a variety of reasons. It remains on the air for one reason: It works. Never doubt it. If an ad doesn't disappear, that usually means it's selling the stuff. The same old formulas recur, decade in and decade out, with the same old results—scores and sales. Marge and Ethyl wouldn't be summoned back time and again if they didn't keep whupping competitors in copy tests. Their winning formula? Conflict. Marge uses Product A, Ethyl insists that Product B is better. A conflict situation. But then, isn't all literature and all drama filled with just that, conflict situations? Conflict commercials are microdramas, and viewers tend to get involved. And to remember the situation next day when Burke Testing calls. Of course if they remember the conflict, chances are they'll remember the resolution. Ethyl's product bested Marge's product in the cutaway demonstration. Product B is a better buy.

There are two formula endings common to conflict commercials, the Easy Lay and the Chuckler. If the opponent, having championed Product A at the outset, 12 seconds later embraces Product B ("I'm convinced! I'll switch to new Bold!"), that's an Easy Lay. If the adversaries join in consensus at the end, and find that cause for hilarity, like this:

BRENDA: Let's fill it to the rim.
BOB: With Brim. (Both laugh)

That's a Chuckler. I never did grasp the full merriment of filling it to the rim, but that's just me.

Does conflict score big every time? No, but it scores so often that rarely is a range of new commercials tested without a conflict entrant. Which triumphs often enough to keep Marge and Ethyl comparing wash in perpetuity. In fact, what remains, I believe, the highest-scoring commercial in P&G history is an early spot for Folger's Coffee. The wife calls the husband in for coffee. He takes one sip and dumps it in the sink. "You call that coffee? I call it terrible!" *Ding!* Big score. Did women feel bad for the wife? Some did, but most thought it served her right for serving terrible coffee.

Which brings us to formula two. Conflict is always good, but seldom as good as good old-fashioned guilt, expertly wrought. The accusing finger points at the wife or mother in the film, but by transference at you, the viewer. Roger and his wife emerge from the shiny silver plane and they're greeted by a beautiful wahine girl. "Welcome to Hawaii," she says, laying a lei on Roger's neck. But then—organ chord in minor key—she recoils, pointing. "Ooh, ring around the collar." Whose fault? Roger's fault? No, Roger's *wife's* fault. (Cut to her, devastated.) If she'd only used Wisk. She will next time. Will you?

There are half a dozen time-corroded-but-honored formulas for composing television advertising. Every hack copywriter has a file of them which he opens upon request for a new campaign. They are

Conflict

Guilt

Testimonials ("Mrs. A. J. of Boston says . . . ")

Candids ("Will your husband prefer mashed potatoes or Stove Top?")

Graphic Demonstration ("Ordinary nasal sprays free only *some* sinus cavities. . . . ")

Spokesperson (the Pathmark guy in the blue suit and hard hat)

First Person Singular ("I'm brushing my breath, with Dentyne")

Celebrity (We've discussed.)

The Owner on the Air (We will discuss.)

Shouting

Ah, shouting. All you folks located outside Crazy Eddie's raving range, signify by raising your right hand and whispering Thank God. You probably have hysterical TV merchants of your own, but Crazy Eddie was, I think, the first and remains the foremost. Goes like this: A chubby party in jacket and turtleneck jumps out from behind a store counter, waving his arms like he's calling the fire trucks, and shouts at you, correction, screams at you:

> CRAZY EDDIE'S EVERYDAY PRICES PUT OTHER STORES' SALES
> PRICES TO SHAME! TVS, STEREOS, RECORDS, TAPES, AT BELOW
> WHOLESALE COSTS! CRAZY EDDIE'S PRICES ARE *INSANE!*

Your eardrums throb, your eyes water, your nerves are frazzled, but you did get the message. The thought is, there's so much advertising clutter on television, in order to succeed you've got to be intrusive. I'll give Crazy Eddie that, he is successful and he is intrusive. I wonder, is it against the law to shoot an intruder?

Now about the primitives selling storm windows. There's a dog-eared bit of doggerel, composed long ago by a copywriter who'd lost all illusions, about keeping a difficult client happy. It's as relevant today as it was 70 years ago when Guy Gillette took to the magazine pages to hawk his razor blades.

> *When the client moans and sighs,*
> *make his logo twice the size.*
> *If he still should prove refractory,*
> *show a picture of his factory.*
> *Only in the gravest cases*
> *should you show the clients' faces.*

Gravest case #1. Your biggest client is about to walk. If he walks, he takes half the agency revenue with him. You've tried every which way to please him, but nothing works. Conflict situations, guilt, testimonials, candids, every formula in the file has failed and—wait a minute. Of course! This one can't fail!

Gravest case #2. You're pitching a new account but you know deep down that your chances are slimmer than zero. The other contending agencies have fuller service to offer, better marketing, keener critical insights. You've got what? You've got a nerve even thinking about winning . . . wait a minute! Of course! What can blow right by insight, service, and marketing and steal the race? Vanity.

Owner vanity. He founded the company, didn't he? Yes. Is he proud of it? Very. He's a salesman, isn't he? One of the best. Good on his feet? Very good. Would he love to stand in front of a television camera in his best suit and a hundred-dollar haircut and tell the whole world about his product? You bet he would.

That's just what you're doing, betting he would. You make your move.

YOU: Tony, I'll never forgive myself. Here I've been searching all over creation for the right way to sell this product and it's been there all the time, right in front of my eyes. What could be righter than having the man who *makes* the product *talk* about the product! Who knows more about it? How it's made, the quality that goes into it, the importance of it in people's lives. Who better than you?

TONY: Hey, I'm no actor. I'm just an ordinary guy.

YOU: Perfect! An ordinary guy talking to ordinary people! Not some slick salesman in a shiny suit, a real flesh-and-blood guy talking one-on-one, straight from the shoulder, about an extra-special product! I love it! What do you say?

TONY: I don't know. Maybe you got something there.

You devil. Tony falls for it and the account is yours. Well done. How is Tony on the air? Of course he's terrible, and yet he's not. Because there was some truth in that rasher of baloney you sold him. He is so totally unprofessional that he stands out by contrast, and that isn't all bad. He obviously does believe in his product and sincerely wants viewers to believe in it too. And in a strange way, they do.

Example: There's a storm-window company in New Jersey that advertises in the off hours on the New York off channels, but watch enough television and sooner or later you'll catch the spot. Center screen there's a storm window with dollar bills blowing through it, scattering all about. Next to the window stands the company owner in his best suit, intoning this admonition:

Home owniz! Stop trowin ya hod-earned cash out da winda!

Primitive? Amateurish? Call it what you want, but you will recall the little man with the blowing bills when you think about storm windows. Will you buy his windows? That's another story. Would better advertising sell more windows? That's still another story. It has been said, more than once, that the only bad advertising is advertising that doesn't sell. Do we buy that? No. Whether it sells or not, bad is bad, and yes, I do firmly believe that better advertising would sell more windows.

Will you be obliged to open the formula file at times during your career? Probably all too many times. When you do it, try to bring something new to it. A good many times, you can.

Just promise me one thing. Promise me solemnly that you will never ever do a Crazy Eddie commercial.

13

PEOPLE METERS

Remember our hamlet of a hundred homes where 22 of the TVs were dialed to *Dynasty?* Well, in 1986, Nielsen reported that 22% of the whole nation's TVs were dialed to *Dynasty.* That 22 rating was keenly pleasing to ABC sales execs because it allowed them to charge $150,000 for one 30-second time slot in the show. Which in turn was keenly pleasing to agency media folks because it allowed them to buy time in a hit show for a commendable CPM of $8.00 (85 million TVs × 22% = 19 million;

$150,000 ÷ 19,000 (thousands of viewers) = $8.00 CPM). Which in turn keenly pleased the agencies' clients because it allowed them to offer their wares to millions of prospects at reasonable cost.

Neat arrangement? Very neat. Providing the 22 was accurate. Pause just a moment and consider the weight of the structure balancing on that little number: The fate of a big-time network show, its renewal or cancellation *and therefore the fates of competitive shows,* the money ABC received for advertising sold in the show, which paid not only for the show but for ABC's rent, paper towels, and hall pictures too, the careers of agency media people along with the fortunes and futures of their agencies, the sales of the products advertised, therefore the jobs and lives of the marketing and creative people at the agencies and the client companies too, *all of this* teetered, like Atlas on one toe, on that number 22.

Well just a moment, you say, do we *know* the 22 was accurate or don't we? And if we do, *how* do we know? Good question. I mean, no one phoned *me* and asked what *I* was watching. Did anyone phone you? About any show, ever? No. We know because Nielsen told us so. A. C. Nielsen Inc., the nation's pollster. And Nielsen knew because 4300 families told them so. As you read this description of the Nielsen system you will realize clearly that polling a nation, like selecting a spouse, is a very inexact science. Understand first that no pollster can ever poll everybody. So they create what in research lingo is called a sample universe. That is, a few thousand people selected to represent the rest of us in age, sex, region, and wealth. Nielsen contracted with 1700 families to install TV meters in their homes. Whenever the sets were on, the meters recorded time and channel. What they didn't record was who was watching the programs. Advertisers need to know that. They need to separate their prospects from the populace by the choice of shows they sponsor. Levi's jeans, for instance, doesn't care if Mom, Pop, Uncle Dennis, Baby Faye, and Bingo the dog are all watching *Dallas.* If teenage Tina is upstairs watching *Miami Vice,* that's where Levi's wants to be. Hanes doesn't care about Dad and Uncle Dennis, Miller Beer doesn't care about Mom and Tina, and so on.

And that's supposing anyone was watching at all! How many times did Mom go next door and leave the set on CBS? The meter recorded a score for *All My Children* with nobody but Bingo on the couch.

So Nielsen contracted with 2600 other families to keep *diaries* of who watched what. Every week someone, usually Mom, mailed in the information. Then the diary home stats were correlated with the meter home stats and the nation's television ratings were determined. All those 22s and 31s and 14s, on which all those programs, media plans, budgets, personal careers, zip codes, and home lives depended.

Well, okay, given the inexactitude of polling, what was wrong with the Nielsen system? Plenty, its critics insisted. For one thing, the sample universe was not truly representative of the rest of us. The families tended to be older and more rural. Younger urbans were underrepresented and so, therefore, were their shows. Too often programs they favored died unmerited deaths.

For another, the diary reporting was flawed by human nature. The diarist, usually Mom, usually waited till the end of the week, then tried to think back to who watched what. Let's see, what did we watch Tuesday? It must have been *Moonlighting* . . . we usually watch *Moonlighting* . . . I'll put *Moonlighting.* It so happened that the family watched an NBC special on Tuesday but Mom was busy with Baby Faye for most of it and it slipped her mind. Not surprisingly, Nielsen ratings have always tended to favor middle-age appeal programs and female-appeal programs.

So, back to your question. Was the 22 accurate? Probably not. But how inaccurate was it? Was the right rating 18? 15? 12? If so, that commendable CPM of $8.00 would become something like a dreadful $14.00. And therefore that $150,000 was way too high and therefore all those media plans and all those budgets and all those careers and zip codes were . . . oh my goodness. Which is why, although everybody suspected that the ratings were off, nobody was overanxious to upend the system.

Until recently. The pressure simply grew too great, and it came from two directions. Agency buyers clamored louder and louder for accuracy, but they might be clamoring still if alternate polling systems, competitive to Nielsen, hadn't appeared on the market. Rapidly, some say just in time, Nielsen introduced a new television auditing system. The people meter, in theory, combines the two previous systems for greater accuracy and information. Goes like this: Each member of the family is assigned one button on the meter. Mom is button one, Pop is two, Uncle Dennis is three, Tina is four. He or she enters the room, pushes the button on, watches TV, gets up, pushes the button off, and leaves. Nielsen has data-banked demographics on all members of all 4000 families so they'll be able to provide advertisers exact stats on who watches what by age, region, and income. In theory.

One thing for sure, the new people-meter families are skewed younger and more urban than the previous system's families. That's already having an influence on ratings. Under the old system, *Dallas* regularly trounced *Miami Vice* on Friday nights. In the earliest people-meter samplings, the two shows scored about even. Younger viewers. And some long-held industry verities may be in for some scrambling too. Early evidence shows that women watch less daytime TV and more sports than the old system led us to believe. Again, younger, hipper women.

Now about those competitive systems. One, AGB National TV Ratings Service, stepped forward to challenge Nielsen in 1986. Nielsen hastened to introduce its new system and might have beaten back the AGB challenge if it hadn't been for CBS. CBS took one look at the early people-meter test scores and called a foul on Nielsen. Unfair sampling, they complained—regional bias! CBS shows have always been popular in the South, less so in California. Nielsen, in adjusting from older rural to younger urban, lessened representation in the South and raised it in California. *Falcon Crest, Murder, She Wrote,* maybe even *60 Minutes* would suffer. CBS's income would certainly suffer. CBS acted. In 1987, they fired Nielsen and hired AGB, who presumably promised to place their meters closer to Dallas. We'll see.

All in all, the people meter does seem to bring us one notch nearer exactness in the polling science. But maybe only one. Think about all that button pushing. Would all the people in your family remember their buttons every time? Dutiful Mom probably will, but ditzy Uncle Dennis?

Doubtful. He has a habit of falling asleep in his chair halfway through *The Tonight Show* while the meter runs on and on. . . .

People meters are definitely here to stay, though, and they will grow, over the next decade, even more informative and precise. Because advertisers will insist on even more precise information on who's watching what. There's even talk about a competitor company offering a meter with a built-in heat sensor that can tell when someone enters or leaves the room. But can it tell the difference between Uncle Dennis and Bingo? Stay tuned.

14

*T*HE *P*RESSURE
OF *I*T *A*LL

*M*any of our listeners have written in, asking if it's true that advertising is a pressure business. Yes, indeed it is, and that's something you need to know about. Let me cite some pressure points.

Primarily there's the pressure to perform, to excel day after day. I have two radio commercials to write today and a newspaper ad to supervise. I must do it all today and I must do it very well. There's good creative margin on the radio spots—that is, only a few mandatory points to make and a client who likes to laugh. The pressure is on me to write two radio commercials that sell product and enhance my reputation as a copywriter. My junior writer on the newspaper ad is young and loves to swing for the fence every time. Only this isn't the ad for it. I'll explain to him in my best varsity letterman manner that it's wiser to swing for a solid hit every time and let the home runs fall as they may. Those are my pressures today. Tomorrow's pressures may be more severe, maybe less, but they'll be different.

Then there's the pressure to stay current in a rapidly changing industry, one currently ruffled by local marketing, people meters, budget shrinking, new developments in fashion, music, electronic animation. You keep current with the change or it nudges you off onto a side street.

There's always the pressure to stay ahead of your accounts, to be the initiator of change and not the victim. Satchel Paige's advice never to look back 'cause trouble may be gaining on you is bad advice in this business. Best be looking back, front, left, and right at all times and staying way ahead of trouble, or it will catch you for sure and mash you flat.

Feeling stuck in the wrong job; feeling stifled by the wrong boss; feeling terminal in a dead-end agency; working for a permanently high-anxiety client, like a toymaker; and of course the big one, fear of losing an account; they're all enough to send you home with a baseball in your belly.

Remember that all these dramas are played against the backdrop of scant security. Your only insurance is your skill and your temperament.

Then again there are many pressures other jobs have that this job doesn't have, as well as several nice freedoms it does have. There is obviously no fear of physical injury in advertising. Very few media buyers were killed in the line of duty last year. You never feel the insidious pressure of watching the world pass you by in a futureless job, or the frustration of realizing that on this day 20 years from now you'll be performing essentially the same tasks you did your first day on the job.

Then there's freedom. You come and go more or less as you please. If I finish my two dazzling radio commercials this morning, I'll take a long lunch and run some errands. If I don't, I'll work on them over a sandwich in my office. You dress more or less as you please, if you're creative. If you're account, you probably lay out five white shirts or blouses for the week. You outfit your office more or less as you please. Mine is a living room, all couches and books. Others incline more toward boudoirs, dens, or dentists' offices.

Skill and temperament. Until recently, agency recruiters sought only the first. They're now mining for temperamental affinity as well, realizing that the failure rate has more to do with personality than with brains. There are many very bright young people who view the uncertainties of advertising with misgivings. In all probability, this is not their line. How about you? Are you joyed or dismayed by the prospect of doing something different every day? Of relying on your talent for security? Of changing agencies two or three times in your career? Think it over. It could be the most vital consideration in your decision.

15

Past, Present, and Future Conditional

*I*t was clearer back then. Back when there were a dozen big agencies and a dozen not so big, each one with an identity. At Doyle Dane, creative conquered all, at Wells Rich too and at a few of the not so bigs. At Bates it was heavy (some say heavy handed) marketing; same with Compton and Esty. Young and Rubicam, Ogilvy, BBDO, and most of the centrists offered a balance. So a client had a clear choice. For pure creativity, as with Volkswagen, he went to Doyle. For pure marketing, as with Dristan, he went to Bates. Account and creative people had the same choice. Most clients preferred the balanced middle, and that's where most big agencies strove to be.

No agency represented rival products back then. It was unthinkable, and with reason. An agency, as we've seen, is an extension of the client's marketing arm. Agency and brand people cocaptain the product, sharing plans and information. If an agency should serve two competitive products, there would be two sets of account people, creative people, media people, and in the normal course of rotation, two groups of ex-workers on both products. All sworn to secrecy, of course, but all subject to the normal tendencies toward gossip, anger, mind alteration, boasting, cupidity, even marriage. One way or another, secrets would leak.

So of course every product had its own agency. Every toothpaste, every gasoline, every soap. And in consequence, every agency had its own roster of unrivaled products—one soft drink, one floor cleaner, one auto, one beer. Back then.

Back then advertising revenues rose annually. Year-end figures announced healthy increases of 10%, 15%, 20%, some years even better. It's not hard to see why. Inflation (and greed) increased the prices of clients' products, so their advertising budgets rose. Inflation (and greed) increased the costs of TV time and magazine space. Since an agency's revenue is calculated as a 15% commission on client media spending, agency billings rose by 20% or better every year.

Agencies came to rely on that 20% as a margin for change, a margin for error. There is a normal gain and loss of clients at every agency, as we've discussed. When a client departed, that 20% margin meant that the agency personnel shipwrecked by the loss could be carried until a new account was secured and they were back in business. Marginal employees could be carried for years, out of loyalty or affection. There was always room for one more with those yearly rising revenues. Back then.

Back then, if anything was certain in the world, it was that 15% rate of commission. As certain as the price of gold or the 48 states. Fifteen percent on all media expenses, regardless of how much work was actually involved in servicing the client's needs, which made Wrigley's gum the ideal client. Create one spot, double your pleasure, and run it for five years. A less recompensive client would be one who insisted on a lot of test work. Creating a commercial for test is just as laborious as creating "double your pleasure," and it only runs once. In Syracuse. No cause for concern, though. One Wrigley's covered a host of testy clients. Back then.

Then then became now, and nothing is as it was. Nor will it be again. Or will it? First two agencies did it, then two more did it, then nearly all of them did it. They merged. Sometimes merger was a euphemism for purchase. Some big agencies just flat *bought* little ones. But sometimes it was a genuine merger of two equally big ones. The motivations were different but the consequences were similar.

A big agency bought a little one for one of three reasons. One, for the glitter. That's when the big one was a heavy slow-footed marketing agency, the small one a hot creative boutique. Instant creative credentials. Two, for the business. That's when the small agency served covetable clients that the larger agency couldn't hope to win in the normal come and go. Three, for the reach. That's when the larger agency needed a branch in Houston or Minneapolis to serve a new client. It was easier to buy a branch than to initiate one.

Equal-sizers merged for reasons of reach and efficiency. And, skeptics will add, of empire. Agency One might be weak domestically but strong overseas, Agency Two the reverse. The merged agency combined the strengths and eliminated the weaknesses. Agency Three might be strong in one sort of business, packaged goods for instance, Agency Four in another sort, beer or cars or travel. In merging they created a fuller client roster and fiscal efficiencies as well. One CEO instead of two. One president, one treasurer, one creative director, one mailroom. More efficient condensed departments all around.

Fair enough, but why did the merged merge with the merged to form the megamerged? Just seemed like a good idea? Or was it empire building? Saatchi and Saatchi, an English agency, merged with Backer and Spielvogel plus Dancer Fitzgerald to create a $4.3 billion superagency. Then Doyle Dane Bernbach and Needham Harper merged with

BBDO to form Omnicon, a $5.1 billion superagency. Saatchi and Saatchi, not to be outsupered, merged again, with Bates, to top the industry at $7.5 billion.

Empiricism or imperialism?

However, along with reach and efficiency, all those mergers created a chaos of conflicts. Let's start with the big buying the small. The little agency brought more than creativity to its new parent. It brought at least one rival client, probably two or three. The big agency now found itself with two gins, two banks, two dog foods. One of each had to go, to avoid conflict clashes. Or did they? The boutique is being maintained as a separate, semiautonomous agency, the new owners explained to rival clients, with little exchange between large and small. A conflict is only a conflict, after all, if one or both clients choose to see it as a conflict.

When the big equals began merging, though, scores of obvious conflicts were created, far too serious for either rival to countenance. Oil companies, automobiles, airlines. Some client companies insisted the agency resign one account or the other. Others just shredded their secrets and stormed out.

And where did that leave the personnel who'd been serving the departed client? Mainly on the street. Released with apologies and severance, but released. No agency could afford to shelter four or five entire product groups, even with a plus-20% margin that suddenly wasn't plus any more but minus.

Consider now the dismay of the survivors. But for the accidents of rosters, *they* could have been the jobless. Through no fault but fate's. And who are these new people around here? Didn't we fire her last year? Now she's my supervisor? Then the efficiency firings began. First the duplicates, then the marginals, then the not so marginals. Morale sunk to the mud.

And what happened to that unfailing 20% minimum rise in revenues? In 1986, for the first year in the modern era, advertising revenues rose only 7.6%. Why? The term is disinflation. Costs stopped rising. The costs of clients' merchandise stayed about the same, so advertising budgets stayed about the same. Media costs stayed about the same, so media billings stayed about the same. Profits of 7.6% and sinking don't offer

AGENCY PAYCHECKS

Each year the magazine *Adweek* conducts a salary survey. Here are the results for 1987. These are industry-wide averages, not including bonuses or other benefits.

POSITION	AVERAGE SALARY, IN THOUSANDS
CREATIVE	
copywriter, art director	27.8
supervisor	34.7
creative director	73.3
ACCT. MANAGEMENT	
asst. account exec.	19.4
account executive	32.3
account supervisor	45.0
management supervisor	74.2
MEDIA	
asst. buyer, planner	19.4
buyer, planner	25.0
supervisor	32.0
director	61.7

much of a margin for change, even less for error. There was no more room for one more. Round two of firings came, and this one hurt. Morale was now covered with mud.

The third permanent fixture to fall was the 15% commission. It seemed to fall suddenly. (Just 100 pages ago, you and I were getting our 15% from Friar's.) In fact, client management had been reconsidering agency compensation for some time. Now nearly all corporations are insisting on reduction: 14%, 13%, and the pressure continues. General Motors, it's said, wants ultimately to pay no more than 9%. In recompense, clients are increasing fees for test work. Test advertising used to be, back then, a low-profit or no-profit venture for agencies. That's changing. The coming arrangement seems to be a lower commission with higher fees, which will aid some agencies but injure others. Oh, for those Doublemint days again.

And what about all those conflicts? Some were rapidly resolved, as clients jerked their business the day the merger was announced. Other clients have been waiting and watching, going along for the moment with the agency contention that there is no true conflict if the partners don't share secrets. Many large companies, though, are leaning away from that argument.

In late 1986 a major spender's CEO announced he would not sit still for any agency arrangement that put a competitor anywhere under the same agency roof, no matter how broad that roof might be.

Nor was his merger criticism limited to conflicts. "I hear the arguments about global reach and keeping up with merging clients," he said, "but I'm unconvinced. I simply do not believe that creativity or reach will improve." He was very concerned about the effect of mergers on agency employees, possibly breeding "dislocation and disaffection, uncertainty and underperformance. Not to mention plain fear."

The marketing chief at Kraft agrees on conflicts: "It is extremely difficult to accept an agency as a true partner if another part of the organization is competing with you and hitting where it hurts."

Another marketing chief agrees on mergers in general: "I want agency people who can say their only boss is the client, not another larger agency."

And yet that big spender's CEO wants his agencies to run extremely lean and to "do more with less." And here the president of a large merged agency agrees with him. "We will continue," he announces, "to drive forward toward greater efficiency and strong margins, which means inevitably that we will perform our services for clients with fewer people."

Our CEO would seem to want it both ways. Doing more with less does inevitably mean firing people and insisting the survivors work harder. Which leads inevitably to uncertainty and fear.

For a while.

And that's where you come in. Into a business that has taken a hard hit and lived. Lived to flourish again. Those conflicts will sort themselves out. Probably to the advantage of smaller independent agencies, not necessarily in New York, that will add staff and become full service. They will welcome those refugee conflict clients. The new agencies will, with the help of their new client partners, grow and prosper. Just as the first generation of agency giants did.

Advertising will learn to live on 7% margins, but more permanent fixtures will fall in the process. Some departments will be phased out. Other services, such as casting, will be allocated to outside companies. Travel will be more restricted, lunches less lavish. The business will never be quite the same again, even if inflation hits double digits again. But it will always be quite a business to make your life and fortune in.

Quite a business indeed.

Good fortune to you.

ABOUT THE AUTHOR

*E*d Caffrey has been a copywriter and a creative director at four agencies: Young & Rubicam, Benton & Bowles, Grey, and, most recently, DMB&B. He is now ideating on special projects for General Foods.